The Forgotten Lifeboats of

This book is dedicated to the brave men who manned
the lifeboats at Tyrella, for whom there is no memorial or
plaque acknowledging their service.

"In all generations, lifeboatmen have always been ordinary men doing an extra-
ordinary job; it is the fact that they do get wet, cold, exhausted and sometimes
frightened and are still prepared to go out again that makes them special."

Ray Kipling (1982) p3

Acknowledgements

I should like to thank the RNLI, particularly Hayley Whiting and Nathan Williams for their patience with my many queries and their help in getting the right source material; thanks also to Briege Stitt in the Heritage Gallery of Downpatrick Library, for her help with the micro-fiche reader and the many hidden little gems of information she uncovered for me; a very special thank you to Dan McQuillan for the cover design, taken from one of his own photographs. I owe a massive debt of gratitude to the 'Tyrella Coastguard Crew', Dan, Deirdre, Graham, Kate, and Lyn, for their endless support and encouragement, and for their helpful comments, queries and suggestions on the various drafts. It goes without saying that any errors are mine entirely.

B Lomas, December 2019

Published by: bird rock press [birdrockpress@gmail.com]
Author: Barbara Lomas
Design by: April Sky Design, Newtownards
Printed by: GPS Colour Graphics, Ltd

© Bird Rock Press 2019
ISBN: 978-1-5272-5450-3

Contents

List of Maps

List of Diagrams

List of Illustrations

Lifeboat *p81*]

24. Lifeboatman with lifebelt. [*The Lifeboat 15 May 1875, Volume 9, Issue 96 p274 RNLI Archives*]

25. Brighstone Grange ON 226 self-righting class 'Worcester Cadet'. Lifeboat on carriage being pulled up the beach by horses and helpers with crew on board in cork lifejackets. [*RNLI Archives*]

26. Pounding surf, Tyrella. [*Author's own photograph*]

27. Tyrella Coastguard Station. Row of seven terraced cottages built in 1865 adjacent to the Watch House, on the rocky basalt outcrop of Ringsallin Point, Co Down. [*Author's own photograph*]

28. Falmouth Station. Self righting class 1866 'City of Gloucester'. Lifeboat on horse-drawn carriage on beach with crew in cork lifejackets standing on board. [*RNLI Archives*]

29. List of Subscriptions for Tyrella Branch of the RNLI. [*The Lifeboat 1 April 1861, Volume 4, Issue 40, RNLI Archives*]

30. List of Subscriptions for Tyrella Branch of the RNLI. [*The Lifeboat 15 May 1875, Volume 9, Issue 96, RNLI Archives*]

31. Memorial in Tyrella parish church to Rev. TF Martin, Rector 1858–1878 Erected by the parishioners. [*Author's own photograph*]

32. Close-up obverse shot of Silver Medal for gallantry; Medal on black background. [*RNLI Archives*]

33. Shipwreck Auction Notice. [*Newspaper image © Successor copyright holder unknown, with thanks to the British Newspaper Archive www. britishnewspaperarchive.co.uk*]

34. Excerpt from the Service Book on the Memorial 13 April 1878–24 December 1881. [*Service Book 2 Tyrella RNLI Archives*]

35. Cromer. Liverpool class boat, ON 514, *Alexandra*. Wreck of the Dover barge *Sepoy of Cromer*, Norfolk in December 1933. Firing a rocket to the wreck. Cromer pulling and sailing lifeboat is about to launch.

36. Rocket Launcher. From a composite picture on Lifesaving Apparatus. [*J C Dibdin, Book of the Lifeboat p387*]

37. Hurrah for the Lifeboat crew. [*J C Dibdin, Book of the Lifeboat p215*]

38. Snowstorm at Tyrella with Smith's Rock in the background. [*Author's own photograph*]

39. Courtown Station Self Righter *Alfred & Ernest*, 12 oars, crew aboard wearing cork lifejackets at entrance to boathouse c1860's. The boathouse and background bear a striking resemblance to Tyrella; this was the photograph used by the RNLI in a 2014 tweet *#OnThisDay 140 years ago: Tyrella lifeboat rescued 6 from wreck. Silver*

The Lifeboat

"Been out in a lifeboat often?" "Ay, ay Sir, oft enough."

"When its rougher than this?" "Lor' bless you, this ain't what we call rough,

It's when there's a gale a blowin' and the waves run in a break

On the shore with a roar like thunder and the white cliffs seem to shake;

When the sea is a hell of waters and the bravest holds his breath

As he hears the cry for the lifeboat his summons maybe to death.

That's when we call it rough sir; but, if we can get her afloat,

There's always enough brave fellows ready to man the boat."

(Verse 1 of *The Lifeboat* written in 1883)

George Robert Sims (1847–1922)

Introduction:
The Forgotten Lifeboats of Tyrella

The Royal National Lifeboat Institution is dedicated to saving lives at sea (and inland waters). Its logo is one of the most recognisable in the British Isles and it regularly features in the Top Ten of the UK's best-known charities. It has stations all over the British Isles, including the Republic of Ireland. Some of the RNLI stations can trace their origins back to the earliest days of the charity, some, like Kingstown (Dun Laoghaire), Co Dublin, even before the Royal National Institution for the Preservation of Life from Shipwreck was founded in 1824; other stations like Bangor, Co Down are more recent, reflecting the changing use of the maritime and inland waterways around the British Isles.

The first Lifeboat sent to Ireland under the auspices of the newly formed Royal National Institution for the Preservation of Life from Shipwreck was dispatched to Dundrum Bay in Co Down in 1825 and stationed at Rossglass at the north-eastern end of the Bay; other lifeboat stations followed until, by the end of the 19th century, there were eight stations covering the eastern and northern shores of Ireland. Many of these stations have been closed and others opened in their place as changing technologies meant that motor-driven boats could cover much greater areas than the 'pull and sail' boats of the early and mid 19th century. Histories for the closed former RNLI stations can be found on line and some former stations have preserved their Service Boards and Service Books recalling the 'shouts' or call-outs of the lifeboats stationed there over the years.

However, for one station in the north-east of Ireland there is virtually no mention anywhere… Tyrella in Co Down. Local history books of the area have no record, and the closest RNLI station, just 6 miles away at Newcastle, Co Down, has no reference to it in its online history profile, mentioning only Rossglass, the first lifeboat station in Dundrum Bay. There is a brief mention in the online history of Ballywalter Station, on the Ards peninsula, opened in 1866 (and closed in 1906) but it is largely dismissive of a station existing at Tyrella:

> The reference in the RNLI records of the Ballywalter Lifeboat in 1866 to a lifeboat station existing at Tyrella, rather than at Newcastle, tends to support some evidence that a secondary RNLI lifeboat may have been operating again in the Rossglass/Tyrella area during 1866. It is also possible that an error was made in referring to Tyrella rather than Newcastle in the RNLI 'Lifeboat Journal' of 1866. (i)

Map 1: Dundrum Bay, Newcastle, Tyrella and Ballywalter

Clearly the existence of an RNLI station at Tyrella was not a well-known fact. A 1965 piece by HISTORIA in the *Irish News* displayed a flair for the dramatic in its description of the dangers of Dundrum Bay to sailing ships in the 18th and 19th centuries but it was less than accurate in its coverage of the Rossglass & Tyrella lifeboats, mixing up names, venues and personnel (ii). A much more accurate piece about the Tyrella lifeboats appeared in the local newspaper, the *Down Recorder* in 1992. The article concluded:

The life-span of the Tyrella lifeboat service may have been short but its impressive record shows that it was a much needed service in the days when wrecks were an all too common occurrence in Dundrum Bay. (iii)

Tyrella, Co Down had a lifeboat from 1838–1852, stationed at the Coastguard Watch House, operating under the auspices of the Royal National Institution for the Preservation of Life from Shipwreck; it then became a fully functioning RNLI station operating from 1860–1899, with a Branch Committee, a well-built Lifeboat House and a total of four lifeboats spanning its duration as an active station. The station is credited with saving well over 100 persons from shipwreck and was awarded several RNLI gallantry medals. No Service Boards or Service Books from the Tyrella station have been found to date; a single photograph, sent in by a reader and published in March 1992 in the *Down Recorder*, shows a lifeboat being loaded onto her carriage in Downpatrick, c1860's. This may well be the only surviving photograph of any of the Tyrella lifeboats.

This is the story of the 'Forgotten Lifeboats of Tyrella' and the brave men who risked their lives to save others. All the information for their story, written and visual, has come from contemporary news articles and books, Lloyd's Lists and RNLI Archives; all source material is referenced in Chapter Footnotes found at the end of the book.

(1) Tyrella Lifeboat being loaded onto her carriage in Downpatrick, Co Down c1860's.

Chapter One:
The Dangerous Bay

Tyrella is a civil parish that lies on Dundrum Bay, Co Down, some six miles from the inland county town of Downpatrick and roughly equidistant between Newcastle and St John's Point. The public beach at Tyrella Strand has held the coveted Blue Flag Award since 2011, has a manned RNLI Lifeguard Station during the summer months and is a favourite haunt of wind-surfers who make the most of its exposed position to the southerly and south-easterly winds which frequently whip across its shores. With twenty-five hectares of sand-dunes, it continues to enjoy its 'Area of Outstanding Natural Beauty' and 'Area of Special Scientific Interest' designations, with protected plant species, one of the largest common seal colonies in Northern Ireland and is a haven for wintering or migrating birds such as Brent Geese, Sanderling and Shell-duck.

However, in the 18th and 19th centuries, the coastline around Tyrella, stretching from St John's Point to Dundrum Inner Bay had much less welcome visitors, especially in the regular southerly

Map 2: Walter Harris Map 1743

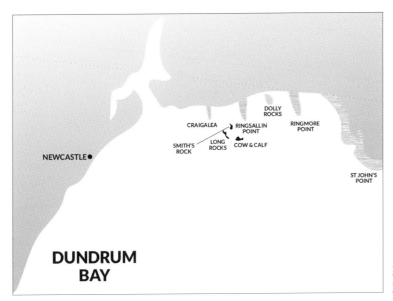

Map 3: Rocky Outcrops, NE Dundrum Bay

gales… sailing ships, driven ashore on its isolated beaches.

Some of these ships were successfully re-floated, but many were pounded to pieces by the relentless breakers. An even worse fate was suffered by the sailing ships that smashed against the long rocky basalt outcrops and reefs which stretch like fingers into the Bay, particularly at the north-eastern end. These were often impossible to see in a full or half full tide, especially in bad weather or at night, until a ship had driven into them; few survivors came ashore from these wrecks.

From the earliest records available, Dundrum Bay had the reputation for being a ship's graveyard. The noted local historian of the 1860's, John Hanna, wrote a series of weekly articles for the *Downpatrick Recorder* called 'Gossipings about…' and he noted:

The Bay of Dundrum, anciently called Lough Rury, then Holie Bay, has long acquired the evil reputation of being a doomed sea, whose rocky barriers, stormy waves and insatiable in-draft have hugged in their treacherous and deadly embrace many a noble vessel to its destruction and become the death bed of many a noble and enterprising mariner. The Irish Annalists record that, in AM 2545, Rury, King of Ireland was here drowned, from whence the name came; and that in AD 922, 1200 of the Northern Corsairs perished in this fatal bay. Year after year the same terrible disasters were repeated. In the 17th century we find the Lords Antrim and Ardglass, among others, cast away; while in the year 1795,

(2) Dundrum Bay from Ringsallin Point at low tide, half tide and full tide.

in the short space of 6 weeks, no less than 26 vessels went to pieces on the shores… In more recent times a fearful catalogue appeared in the columns of the Recorder (December 1839) of upwards of 100 vessels perished within the preceding 40 years. Not a foot of the shore from St John's Point to Annalong but has from time to time been strewn with the broken masts and timbers of Royal and merchant ships, with the spoils and triumph of commerce. (i)

Not only did sailing ships have to contend with the dangerous submerged reefs and frequently shifting sandbanks, but the Bay lacked a natural current to help a ship escape from the frequent southerly or south-easterly gales. A natural occurrence, some five miles south-west of St John's Point (almost opposite Tyrella) was the coming together of the two tides of the Atlantic – one sweeping up from the Irish Sea, the other coursing down from the North Channel. This resulted in the landward side of the confluence being dead water, and ships, driven by southerly gales into the Bay, became embayed and were unable to escape. If the gale was not too severe, the ship could drop anchor and hope to ride out the storm until the wind shifted and allowed them to beat out again. More often than not, the ship was either driven onto the rocks or grounded deep into the sand. Harris, in 1744 noted:

> The Bay is three leagues in length and one and a half in breadth….The North and South tides meeting off this Bay and breaking upon St John's Point occasion a greater eddy or suction inwards than in other places, for many ships have found themselves embayed there, when they were thought to be out in the Channel and if they are once embayed there in a southerly or south-easterly wind, they have no tide to help them out, being sudden among the breakers. (ii)

In 1971, a short book compiled from articles previously printed in the *Mourne Observer* noted:

> The following description of Dundrum Bay, taken from a Lifeboat Journal of about 100 years ago, gives a good idea of how perilous this favourite place can be in a South-Easterly storm: "Dundrum Bay is a deep and dangerous Bay, situated in the centre of the eastern coast of Co Down, facing the south-east, terminating at its north- eastern extremity in St John's Point, and in southerly gales exposed to very heavy seas. The south-western side of the Bay is overshadowed by the Mourne Mountains, which rise to a height of 2,450 feet. On the north and east sides, the shores are flat and shallow, with sands extending to a distance of a mile uncovered, or with a little water on them at low tide, but with a fair depth up to the low shore at high water, so that an ordinary coaster running into the Bay before a south-easterly gale may drive nearly up to the low sandhills at the top of high water, and unless the season be very inclement, the crew can generally save themselves by taking to the rigging till the tide falls, when they may get on shore in safety as the ship, being on moderately hard sand will not go to pieces readily or be engulfed as if on quicksand. But if the tide be not high, a disabled vessel will strike some distance out and the sea, curling over the bulwarks will sweep off the hatches, fill the ship and in several

(3) Drone photograph of Dundrum Bay (Phil Crothers)

cases has caused the total loss of vessels. In these cases, the crew are in imminent danger of being swept away by the overwhelming seas on the return of the tide, if not speedily rescued by the lifeboat." (iii)

The Bay had earned its reputation for being dangerous to sailing ships; as the tonnage of shipping using the Irish Sea and North Channel increased in the 18th and 19th centuries, it is unsurprising that the number of shipwrecks and groundings increased as well. The reason for this exponential growth in shipping lay in the mills, mines and factories of the newly industrialising Black Country.

The end of the Napoleonic Wars ushered in an era of prosperity for Britain. It was not long before the mother country was sucking in raw materials from all over the world – timber and furs from Canada, cocoa and palm oil from Nigeria, tobacco and copper from Rhodesia, teak and jute from Malaya, wool and beef from Australia – and spewing out in return the products of the Industrial Revolution – woollens and cottons and a vast range of machinery and machine-made items. (iv)

This was all conducted within the Mercantilist framework of the Navigation Acts, which stipulated that all commodity trade should take place in British ships, manned by British seamen, trading between British ports and those within the Empire. Any countries, including the colonies, that wanted to trade with Britain had to use British ships to import or export the goods. Exports from Ireland were mostly cattle and linen, while imports were slates and coal, cheaply available from the west coasts of England, Wales and Scotland. Trade routes from Dublin

Map 4: Shipping Routes and Ports on the Irish Sea.

and Belfast to Whitehaven and Troon for cheap coal and North Wales for slates were amongst the busiest on the Irish Sea. Tea, sugar and tobacco brought into Ireland had huge tax levies or tariffs which encouraged smuggling, particularly rife on the coastal area from Dundrum to the Ards Peninsula, with its proximity to the Isle of Man, which, until its purchase in 1765 by the British Government from the Duke of Atholl, was a smuggler's lair. During the 18th and 19th centuries Ireland's dependence on Britain for trade grew; 45.7% of Irish exports went to Britain in 1700, by 1800 the figure was 85.4% and growing yearly.

The huge increase in trade saw a rise in the number of ships that made use of British and Irish ports, leading to a corresponding growth in the number of shipwrecks around the coast of the British Isles. Records of shipwrecks for this period rely on returns made by local agents to Lloyd's Insurers and on reports in local newspapers. Naturally *Lloyd's Lists* did not include ships that were un-insured and small ships such as coasters, colliers and fishing smacks would not normally have warranted a mention in the local newspapers of the time. These reports of ships lost were almost entirely focused on the loss of capital – the ship and its cargo; the fate of the crew was, at best, an afterthought. The name of the vessel, its Master, route and cargo along with its fate or likely fate made up the only information published; there was an occasional two-word epitaph of '*crew perished*' or '*crew saved*'. The growth of maritime trade rolled on, regardless of losses, still less the cost of human lives.

The capital losses sustained by shipwreck slowly began to come to the attention of Parliament; figures were prepared by the Board of Trade for the total number of shipping casualties along the entire coastline of the United Kingdom and submitted to Parliament. They showed a total for the year 1850 of 692 vessels wrecked, and in 1851 of 701. This rose in 1852 to 1,115 ships lost, of which a huge proportion were colliers. "In other words, a ship was being driven ashore and battered to destruction almost every six hours" (v). The first edition of *The Lifeboat*, the new journal of the re-invigorated RNLI was published in 1852; it commented:

> When we consider that, in addition to the cross-channel trade, the whole of foreign trade
> to Liverpool, Glasgow and Belfast passes through the Irish Sea, the frequency of wrecks
> on the east coast of Ireland need not cause surprise. (vi)

Most larger vessels using the North Channel or coming up the Irish Sea to Liverpool, Glasgow or Belfast chose to sail on the western side of the Isle of Man because of the depth of water, as shown in the diagram below. The increased shipping in the Irish Sea and the dangerous nature of Dundrum Bay to sailing ships caught in a southerly or south-easterly gale, resulted in a large number of ships being grounded or wrecked in the Bay. The toll of ships lost (1747–1897) along the eight miles of coastline from St John's Point to Dundrum Inner Bay can be calculated from contemporary sources to be at least 215. The peak period of losses was from 1825–1885, reflecting the huge increase in the volume of shipping up and down the Irish Sea and the North Channel.

A table showing the ships, routes, cargo and the fate of crew and ship, gleaned from contemporary sources (1747–1897) can be found in Appendix 1. Appendix 2 gives a brief description of the sailing ships of the period.

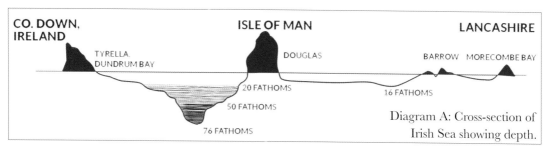

Diagram A: Cross-section of Irish Sea showing depth.

The number of shipping losses in Dundrum Bay also did not go un-noticed in the Irish news journals of the day. Readership of these papers was confined to the educated classes, especially the merchants and ship-owners whose concern for their ships and cargo became more marked as the losses increased. Various suggestions were made in the news-sheets as to how to address these losses along the east coast of Ireland; there was a strong feeling that the problem of shipping losses in Dundrum Bay could be resolved with a lighthouse.

An approach to the Corporation for Improving the Port of Dublin (thereafter to become the Dublin Ballast Board) was made in 1825 from:

> …the principal landholders, merchants, and shipowners being on the coast of the County Down… in connection with the trade of Belfast and the other Northern Ports with Dublin and elsewhere, beg leave to state – "that from our experience for many years past, we conceive that of the many most lamentable shipwrecks that have happened in the Bay of Dundrum, by far the greatest number may [be] attributed to the want of a Lighthouse on St John's Point which forms one of the extremities in that dangerous bay. This much of land being low and extending far into the sea, it is almost impossible even for persons acquainted with the coast, at sight to discern it, and to this circumstance the masters of ships have uniformly attributed their being embayed and their consequent shipwreck… (vii)

The letter was signed by the Marquis of Downshire, Marquis of Donegall, the Earls Roden and Annesley, both MPs for the County Down (Arthur Hill and M Forde) and landowners such as Edward Ward (Castleward) William Ogilvie (Ardglass Castle), George Hamilton (Tyrella House) William Montgomery (Greyabbey) and Andrew Nugent (Portaferry House). It would be hard to think of a more illustrious list of supplicants. However, the Corporation rejected the request:

> …the idea of erecting a Light House on St John's Point is not new to many Members of the Corporation but it has been heretofore overruled in their minds by a consideration of the dangerous disadvantage of multiplying lights on a part of the coast already very largely provided with them… as soon as the season will permit a particular inspection shall be made of St John's Point by the proper officer… (viii)

The multiplication of lights could only refer to the newly erected light house at Haulbowline, at Carlingford Lough (1824) and the already existing Kilwarlin Lighthouse, (known as the South Rock Lighthouse), Portaferry, which had existed since 1797. Whether or not such an inspection

(4) Letter from the Marquis of Downshire and gentlemen (1825).

was carried out, no Light House was built on the Point, and the number of shipwrecks in the 'dangerous bay' continued to grow year on year.

The continuing toll of ships and cargo lost in the Bay ensured that the issue of the Light House never went away; just over ten years later, according to the editorial piece in the *Newry Telegraph*:

> It is the almost universal opinion that the vast number of shipwrecks which have occurred in Dundrum Bay are wholly to be ascribed to the non-existence of a Light-house on the well-known headland of St John's Point… we find that from the year 1831 till the present 1837, a period of only six years, there have been no fewer than 16 vessels driven on shore in Dundrum Bay, the value of which, with their cargoes, reaches the immense sum of £50,000. (ix)

A letter published in 1837 explained why St John's Point was the ideal site for such a Lighthouse:

> St John's Point is the most southerly headland on that coast of Ireland, lying immediately

opposite to the Isle of Man, which considerably narrows the channel between them. It is a point of departure for outward bound vessels, from the British and Irish coasts, as well as from Liverpool, by vessels headed into the Channel by contrary winds; and it is also generally made for by homeward bound vessels, particularly in thick weather, in order to shape their future course up channel. (x)

The issue of a lighthouse at St John's Point became the focus of a vocal campaign by the newly founded (1836) *Downpatrick Recorder* and its editor Conway Pilson. The *Recorder* began to publish accounts of ships lost in the Bay and berated the 'powers that be' for not doing anything about it, such as this impassioned plea:

How much more evidence is wanting? How many more human bodies must become prey of the monsters of the deep, before a lighthouse be erected at St John's Point? How many thousands and tens of thousands worth of property must be lost to the community? Surely the Dundrum coast will not much longer be the altar upon which so many unfortunate seamen are to be immolated (xi)

The new campaign won the support of merchants and important landowners such as Captain PRM Browne of Janeville, on St John's Point, AH Montgomery of Tyrella House, and the Marquis of Downshire. By early 1840 the matter had been conceded, albeit somewhat reluctantly, by the Dublin Ballast Board who, until 1867, had the responsibility for providing Lighthouses on the east coast of Ireland. There is no question that the influence exerted by the Marquis of Downshire was critical in tipping the balance, but the arguments put forward by Leonard Watkins, the Lloyd's agent for Co. Down, the staggering capital costs as indicated in the Newry Telegraph editorial, and the signatures of virtually every merchant and shipowner in Belfast and Liverpool, affirming the commercial importance of such a lighthouse, made the final decision compelling.

The *Downpatrick Recorder* kept the pressure on; after any major shipping loss in the Bay, an editorial would appear, reminding the public of the importance of the Lighthouse, such as this article from 1842:

Although the water in the Bay is of considerable depth it is nevertheless very dangerous, especially along the Tyrella and Rathmullan coast. Here it is very rocky, many of which lie from one and a half to two miles from the main land, the greater number of which are under water at about half-tide. Should a vessel therefore running on shore come in contact

(5) St John's Point Lighthouse

with one of these sunken rocks, the fate of the many hundreds who have already perished on them indicates with fearful certainty, the melancholy and fateful result. It might, however, not be altogether out of place to remark that nine-tenths that are either wrecked or stranded in this Bay are driven on shore with wind South or South-East; for vessels in running down the Channel, generally keeping close to the Mourne shore, and St John's Point being low and not easily discerned on a dark and stormy night, they consequently become embayed and fall in upon the lee shore, while it is highly probable they flatter themselves that they are still in the Channel. In such cases, therefore, the proposed Lighthouse will be of unspeakable service in marking the entrance to the Bay. (xii)

The new Lighthouse at St John's Point opened for business in 1844, and its warning beacon was important to ships navigating the Channel; however, its presence did not magic away the dangers in Dundrum Bay, it merely lessened them. As long as ships relied purely on sail for propulsion, the combination of a southerly or south-easterly gale and the total lack of a natural current, caused by the confluence of the two Atlantic tides only five miles out into the middle of the Bay, ensured that many sailing ships would become embayed, with all the attendant risks of shipwreck.

Chapter 2:
Enter the Lifeboats

The end of the Napoleonic Wars in 1815 not only saw the burgeoning of the Industrial Revolution, but also the start of a century when man's concern for those less fortunate than himself began to become more evident. One in every four mariners who went to sea, died at sea, a higher mortality rate than any other occupation at the time, including mining. Human error and bad weather were sometimes compounded by unscrupulous ship owners, who would dangerously over-load ships in order to make as much profit as possible. There were many incidents of owners over-insuring their vessels, and then sending them to sea in such poor repair that they were not sea-worthy. If the ships sank, as was likely, the owners claimed back several times their real value in insurance, but the lives of the mariners or passengers on board carried no monetary value and so were not of significance. If a seaman, having signed on, then refused to sail on a ship he considered unseaworthy, he faced imprisonment. Such vessels were known as 'coffin-ships' and merchant sailors lived in fear of crewing them.

The *Downpatrick Recorder* in 1855 carried the following article:

> The frequency of vessels stranding at Tyrella, even after a lighthouse has been erected at St John's Point is regarded by many as a suspicious circumstance. It is believed in fact, and the idea, whether well or ill- founded, has taken firm hold in the minds of some, that vessels are driven on shore after a deliberate plan to wreck them and make money more easily by defrauding the underwriters than by risking the perils of a long voyage… there have been suspicious cases on the shore in question. Vessels have been seen beating about the Channel as if to kill time. It is stated that money has now been distributed among the people resident in the neighbourhood to prevent their making public any ugly facts of which they might have become cognizant. (i)

Whether or not there was deliberate waiting about for a southerly or south easterly storm, it is quite telling that a very respectable regional paper should print the concern.

The following article appeared in 1867 in a Naval Journal:

> A memorial from 170 seamen belonging to the North East ports of the UK has been forwarded to the Registrar General of Shipping for transmission to the Board of Trade,

containing an enumeration of grievances appertaining specially to colliers and coasting vessels. Among the grievances are found the under-manning of ships… that these vessels are very commonly unseaworthy being leaky in the hulls and deficient in canvas and cordage; and that in consequence the pumps are constantly at work and the running gear continually in want of repair, to the exhaustion of the scanty crew employed. (ii)

There was little protection for the merchant seamen until a series of improvements were made to the existing Navigation Acts, which naturally took time to embed in and be enforceable. It was not until 1873 that Samuel Plimsoll MP succeeded in getting Amendments to the Merchant Shipping Act 1854 that established a maximum loading line on the sides of a ship … which became known as the Plimsoll Line.

Shipowners had to make money and seamen were often expendable commodities. The *Weekly Vindicator* printed a story in 1849, concerning four seamen who had volunteered to go off in their ship's boat in search of a fellow crew-member who had slipped off the highest part of the ship's masts and fallen into the sea; the men failed to find him and tried to get back:

Owing to the thickness of the weather, the boat was unable to reach the ship and landed with great difficulty at Tyrella Coastguard Station, where they have been taken care of. They were at sea, in a gale of wind from 1pm to 5pm in an open boat. The vessel, the *Osceola*, put into Belfast Lough on Saturday to ship seamen in place of those who were absent, but did not come to anchor and sailed in the evening. The four men who had volunteered to go in the boat in search of their fallen colleague arrived in Belfast on Sunday, but too late to join the ship on which their clothes and chests are. (iii)

There is no record of what happened to the four sailors, left in Belfast with no clothes other than what they stood up in, or any personal possessions that might have been in their sea-chests and no means of letting the captain know that they were alive so that their sea-chests would not be auctioned off to other sailors. Life for a mariner in the 18th and 19th centuries was often 'nasty, brutish and short'.

The first charity to come to the aid of the shipwrecked mariner was founded in 1824 by Sir William Hillary who had taken refuge in the Isle of Man after a series of failed ventures forced him from public life. Whilst resident there he had witnessed many shipwrecks off the Manx coastline and had been an active participant in several rescue attempts. He made a proposal to the Admiralty in 1823 for an organisation dedicated to saving life as the primary concern in a shipwreck (not the safety of the ship or cargo as was the practice at the time) but was summarily

(6) Colonel Sir William Hillary Bt., founder of RNLI.

turned down. He then turned to men of social standing, with a view to making the organisation a charitable one; because of his overtures a most unlikely triumvirate developed of William Hillary, Thomas Wilson (Liberal MP and a shipping magnate of the West Indies Merchants) and George Hibbert, a Whig MP. Between them they had enough political, business and social influence to convince forty of the 'great and good' to attend the inaugural meeting of the new charity in London… The National Institution for the Preservation of Life from Shipwreck. Chaired by the Archbishop of Canterbury, the Prime Minister of the day, (2nd Earl of Liverpool,) was its President, George IV agreed to be its patron and the Royal Dukes its vice-patrons; it was a glittering array of the most influential and powerful men of the time. The meeting adopted a number of resolutions which still lie at the heart of the RNLI today, principal of which was that the rescue of people, irrespective of their nationality, in war or peace, was the first priority at a wreck or salvage.

The National Institution for the Preservation of Life from Shipwreck (or the 'Shipwreck Institution' as it became known) was one of a large number of charitable foundations that grew up in England after the end of the Napoleonic Wars; profound social changes accompanied the rapid industrialisation of the nation and social consciences, at least amongst the better educated classes, were beginning to develop. Well before the latter end of the century practical assistance for the weak and vulnerable was considered a Christian duty for the middle and ruling classes. However, the State was viewed with massive suspicion and was expected to take no role in assisting those in need, lest they become 'puppets of the system'. Individual voluntary support was considered to be the best way to hold off a potentially over-mighty State; at all costs, personal responsibility must be nurtured, so that people could learn to fend and cope for themselves. It was the polar opposite to the expectations of those who view assistance from the State and 'benefits', as their Right.

The fledgling 'Shipwreck Institution' had no shortage of illustrious supporters or of initial injection of funds, which allowed it to begin building Lifeboats to send around the UK coast where they were needed. However:

> Royal Dukes, Bishops and Archbishops are not renowned for their knowledge of seamanship; several committee members did not know the blunt end of a boat from the sharp end and deliberations tended to be lengthy and conclusions not always the best… for example: the type of lifeboat sent to a particular station was not always suited to local conditions and more often than not no provision was made for its maintenance. (iv)

The Institution wanted to encourage local areas to fundraise to provide their own crews, loosely under the auspices of the Royal National Institution for the Preservation of Life from Shipwreck, which would recognise, with monetary rewards, special efforts made by individuals or crews and would reward outstanding bravery with gold and silver medals.

The idea of a Lifeboat, as a specially designed boat specifically constructed for saving lives at sea was not new; Lionel Lukin received a royal patent from the future George IV in 1785 for his boat with cork and airtight lockers or enclosures under the seats, designed to give the boat greater buoyancy. His claim to have invented the first lifeboat has been shared with William Wouldhave and Mr Henry Greathead. [See Appendix 3 for information on the early lifeboats.] The construction of a boat designed to weather storms in which ordinary open fishing boats could not survive was new and exciting to local groups, who enthusiastically fundraised to build a Boat House, contribute to the cost of the lifeboat and its equipment and pay the ongoing costs of crew and coxswains.

(7) Letter to Marquis of Downshire confirming the establishment of a Co Down Branch.

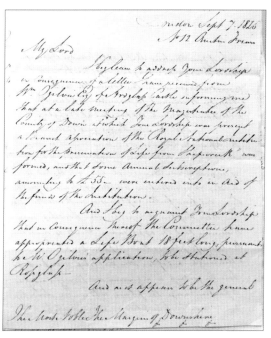

One such local group, the first in Ireland, was centred round the Marquis of Downshire, whose estate in Co Down encompassed the fishing village of Dundrum, where he had built his summer mansion at Murlough House. With his encouragement, a group of local dignitaries and magistrates had contributed funds sufficient to order a boat from the Institution, built by Mr Plenty of Newbury. The Committee had not made any final decision as to where, along the dangerous coastline of Dundrum Bay, the boat should be stationed. However, it would seem that there were competing interests for its site and the final decision was still pending. One of the consortium, William Ogilvie (at that time 82 years old) was so determined to secure it for his preferred site of Rossglass, at the north eastern end of Dundrum Bay some three miles from Tyrella, that he used some of the money raised by the Committee and built a Boat House at Rossglass (which turned out to be too small and had to be demolished and rebuilt when the boat arrived.) He contacted the shipbuilders directly and arranged for the boat to be delivered to Rossglass, without consulting any of the Committee. There was uproar from the rest of the Committee when they were faced with a fait accompli, but the Marquis of Downshire acquiesced, rather than have the business of the Committee made public; so, the first Lifeboat Station for Dundrum Bay was established.

A small Plenty, 18 feet was stationed at Rossglass in December 1825 to help vessels wrecked in the notoriously dangerous Dundrum Bay. Whilst at Rossglass the boat was used for at least three lifesaving missions, one of which involved saving a man from the vessel *Isle of Dundalk* which had been driven ashore at the eastern end of the Bay. (v)

Its first coxswain was Thomas Fahey or Foy, Chief Boatman of the St John's Point Coastguard, who was the recipient of a silver medal from the Institution for his courageous actions in saving the master and one crew member of a Brig, the <u>Usk</u>, carrying coal and parcel goods to Spain from Liverpool, November 1825 (just before the Lifeboat arrived on station.) It was not long after Ogilvie's death in 1832 that the Lifeboat was physically moved about a mile up the coast to a new Boat House, coming under the control of the local landowner, Captain PRM Browne of Janeville. The 'Shipwreck Institution' marked this turn of events by acknowledging the station as Rossglass/St John's Point, but there does not appear to have been any consultation or permission sought before the move. Although the lifeboat was manned with much bravery, the limitations of an open lifeboat, little bigger than a small fishing boat, were more than apparent and it was swamped on several occasions by heavy seas whilst making rescues, its occupants lucky to escape with their lives.

(8) Illustration from *The Lifeboat* 1875.

One such occasion was the rescue attempt made on the 600 ton ship, the *Coeur de Lion* in September 1837, which hit the rocky outcrop called Ringsallin Point, on which was sited the Coastguard Watch House at Tyrella. The normal crew of the lifeboat, all fishermen, were away with the fishing fleet and the Rossglass lifeboat put out with a scratch crew of Coastguards from the St John's Point station and Captain Browne's own farm labourers. The boat was swamped coming up to the ship and the crew of the lifeboat forced to seek refuge on the *Coeur de Lion* itself, from where they were rescued by boats from the Clanmaghery shore. Tragically one of these boats capsized on its return journey to shore and seven people were lost, two of whom were local fishermen. Whilst the newspapers squabbled over which local man had given the most help, awards were given from the Shipwreck Institution to Captain Browne and the Coastguards of Tyrella and St John's Point for their courageous actions. A fund was raised for the widow and families of the two dead Clanmaghery fishermen.

The Rossglass lifeboat serves as a good illustration as to how the National Institution for the Preservation of Life from Shipwreck had been operating.

> …it drew support from only a small and exclusive section of the public. It had come into being as the protégé of aristocratic patrons, most of whom had been happy to make a one-off donation but were unwilling to pledge continuous financial aid. (vi)

What it had was an enthusiastic, well-meaning Committee who saw the purpose of the Institution as providing lifeboats and the Manby rocket-throwing launchers, coupled with the awarding of cash sums and medals for bravery. What it lacked was astute financial acumen and sound administrative practices.

The idea of awarding medals undoubtedly came from the Royal Humane Society who had established the practice of rewarding acts of selflessness with categorised medals… Gold, Silver and eventually Bronze. The 'Shipwreck Institution' acknowledged extra-ordinary acts of bravery with Gold and Silver medals and, as a third category, their Thanks on Vellum (replaced by a Bronze medal by the end of the 19th century). The medals were carefully cast, with the royal effigy one side and the classical pose of the life being saved on the other; the medal was designed to be worn with a ribbon and its award to the ordinary lifeboatman or humble fisherman, in an era of strict class hierarchy, meant as much as a peerage would have done to a socially aspiring industrial magnate. The awarding of a sum of cash to a lifeboat crew or fishermen was "partly because if rescuers lost their lives, their families might suffer poverty and partly because wrecks were still widely considered as legitimate sources of plunder." (vii)

Public interest in the awarding of one particular medal reached almost the mass social

(9) Medals of the RNLI.

hysteria that we see today, reserved for the likes of boy bands and celebrities... silver medals were awarded to Grace Darling and her father, the lighthouse keeper at Longstone Light in Northumberland, for their rescue of the remaining crew of the *Forfarshire*, wrecked during a storm in September 1838. Grace and her father went out in a small rowing boat, for over a mile in fierce seas to reach the ship; it took two trips to save the nine crew and passengers. Grace was just 23, barely five foot tall, and slightly built; she tragically died of consumption just four years later. The national appetite for her story, her likeness and the endless re-telling of her rescue made her Britain's first national heroine.

(10) Grace Darling

However, the public interest in the work of the Institution waned, as no effort was made to capitalise on the public's response to tales of derring-do; by the early 1840's the Institution had run out of steam and was finding it difficult to fund the new boats required or continue the important monetary rewards to crews for service beyond what could be expected. Lifeboat stations were not supervised; many, like Rossglass, had become personal fiefdoms and little was done to ensure inspection or maintenance of equipment or boats.

> A Parliamentary Select Committee… was told in 1843 that there were 85 lifeboats in existence, under numerous authorities and in widely different states of efficiency. (viii)

By then the Rossglass/St John's Point lifeboat had ceased to exist, having been declared unfit for service.

In 1840 the *Northern Whig* reported a meeting held in the Belfast Chamber of Commerce, at which the two guest speakers, Captains Bowie and Skinner RN had come to solicit support for the Royal National Institution for the Preservation of Life from Shipwreck, as the "funds of the Institution had become unequal to afford the usual assistance." In its commentary, the *Northern Whig* was enthusiastically supportive of "this truly philanthropic and eminently useful Association", believing it should "long since have been formed in Belfast" but pleased that "our merchants have now joined it." The concern of the Editor was the growing number of shipwrecks as trade in and out of Belfast increased, and the article ended by his wish for a lifeboat:

> …at Ballyferris Point or near to it as numerous shipwrecks have, within a short time occurred on that dangerous coast; and we are not aware that a lifeboat could be procured in an emergency nearer than Tyrella. (ix)

This was not a mistake, as the following 1840 article clearly shows:

> "Lifeboats and apparatus for the preservation of life from shipwreck are established and kept up by the Royal National Institution at the following two places on the coast of Ireland, Tyrella and St John's Point (x)

In evidence given in 1845 to a Parliamentary Enquiry the claim was made that: "The lifeboat formerly stationed at Newcastle was removed a few years hence to Tyrella, five miles to the north-east, that being the spot where most wrecks take place." (xi) Thom's Directory (1851) provided more detail:

(11) The Watch House, Tyrella.

Tyrella is the place where the Lifeboat is kept at the Coastguard Station; provided and maintained by the Board. The Coastguard commanding officer in charge. The boat is 22 feet long and 9 feet wide with 3 feet 3 inches in depth. The boat's condition – Good. (xii)

Tyrella Coastguard Station was established in 1821, as one of a chain of Preventative Water Guard stations set up to combat smuggling, which at that time was rife along the Irish coast, particularly around the area from Dundrum to the Ards Peninsula. Watch Houses were built roughly every 8-10 miles along the coast and the Preventatives patrolled their designated area from dusk to dawn, both on land and at sea.

It was an extremely effective move; smuggling, while not totally ended, was effectively curtailed and in 1824 the Irish Preventatives became Coastguards, as had happened a year previously in England. James Dombrain, a young naval captain, had masterminded the campaign set up to stop smuggling and had personally selected the site of every station on the east coast of Ireland as he surveyed the whole coast from his ship. He became Inspector-General of Coastguards in Ireland and held the post until his retirement in 1855. He was an enthusiastic supporter of the 'Shipwreck Institution' and had made several recommendations to them for the placing of lifeboats. One such lifeboat was sent to Arklow in 1826 but was never used and in 1830 it was sent to Newcastle, Co Down where it was also never used. It was removed in 1833 to Skerries (not Tyrella as the witness to the Parliamentary Enquiry had believed.) In 1838 the same lifeboat was sent, still unused, to Rosslare, but by 1839 was declared unfit for service and scrapped. This was almost symptomatic of the problems that the 'Shipwreck Institution' had in keeping control of its property once it had been dispatched.

The two organisations, Coastguards and the 'Shipwreck Institution' had more in common than just being founded in the 1820's "while the latter funded the building of lifeboats, the coastguard often provided the manpower to operate them." (xiii) In 1829 the first official Instructions for Coastguards were published; unsurprisingly the first order of business was the prevention of smuggling and the protection of government revenue. However, there was also a section on lifesaving which instructed that:

> …when a wreck takes place on any part of the coast under the charge of the coastguard every individual on the spot or within reasonable distance is to use his utmost efforts to save the lives of the persons on board the vessel, and also to take charge of the vessel and protect such property as may be saved from embezzlement of any kind. (xiv)

Clearly, the two organisations had a great deal in common.

> Because the Institution wanted its lifeboats to be under the control of some kind of local committee and as the Coastguard was deemed able to perform the Committee's role, many of Ireland's early lifeboats were managed and operated by the government body. (xv)

Tyrella was one such early station. James Dombrain had "declared that the ordinary coastguard boat was useless in the area, but his men would gladly maintain and operate a boat converted by Palmer" (xvi) When one became available, he jumped at the chance. The committee minutes of the Royal National Institution for Preserving Lives from Shipwreck (15 November 1838) include this short memo:

> Received letter from J Dombrain of Dublin. It having recently intimated to him by the Commissioner of Public Works of Dublin that a lifeboat under their charge at Kingstown, near Dublin was not required, he had caused it to be removed to Tyrella in Dundrum Bay, where wrecks frequently occur, but that it appears it will not be efficient for the purpose without the stores, particularised in an Estimate enclosed amounting to £19.11.10. (xvii)

(12) Memo in Minutes of RNLI November 1838.

On the face of it, the action was high-handed; no permission was sought by Dombrain to send the boat up North, but there was an implicit assumption that the Institution would meet the cost of the equipment necessary to make it a serviceable lifeboat (which it did.) The source of the boat was the Dublin Board of Works, the equipping and running of it was under the auspices of the Institution but the everyday management was by the Coastguards at Tyrella Station. The boat type was a NC8, being 22 feet long, 7 feet wide, with a draught of about 3 feet. It was launched off a carriage and was stored in an outhouse at the Coastguard Station. It was in service from 1838 to 1852; RNLI records state it had at least 4 launches and saved more than 20 lives.

Its first call out or 'shout' was within a week of its reported arrival in November 1838, one of the worst years for shipwrecks due to the frequency of dreadful storms; over 30 ships were wrecked or driven ashore on the north-eastern part of Dundrum Bay alone.

RNLI Case 674, dated 21 February 1839 outlined the rescue:

The *British Heroine* drove ashore on 29 November 1838 in Dundrum Bay, it blowing a heavy gale of wind. Peter Davis, chief boatman of coastguards, in charge of the Tyrella lifeboat and George Hicks coastguard, with two fishermen, J Doran and C Doran put

No.	Date of award.	Place where wrecked.	Vessels to which the saved persons belonged.	Names of persons saved.	Names of persons to whom awards have been made.	Award.		
674	1839. Feb. 21.	TYRELLA, Dundrum Bay.	Ship, "British Heroine," 600 Tons, Liverpool to Mobile.	—— Atkins, master, and 19 men, being the whole crew. Saved by Life-boat, stationed at Tyrella.	Peter Davis, George Hicks, Coast Guard, John Doran, Hugh Doran, Patrick Doran, W. Mc Cann, fishermen,	6	0	0
					Mr. Strains, Chief Officer,	1	0	0
					George Clark W. Barry, Coast Guard, 10s. each,	1	0	0
						8	0	0

(13) Case of the *British Heroine*.

out in the lifeboat, but from the fierceness of the weather and the boat not being fully manned, they were an hour before they got alongside. Then they took in and brought several of the crew ashore, at which time, Mr Staines, chief officer and five more of the coastguard men went into the boat, which then made a full crew and proceeded to the ship and brought four more of the crew on shore. Then they went off a third time and brought the captain and two men being the last of the crew on shore; thus succeeded at imminent peril of their lives in rescuing twenty persons from their perilous position. Captain Robinson, Inspecting Commander, says the conduct of the parties was in the highest degree commendable, particularly Peter Davis, chief boatman in charge of the Lifeboat, George Hicks of the coastguard and four fishermen, C Doran, M Doran, J Doran and P McCann. (xviii)

The Institution made an award of 1 sovereign each to the six men who first went out in the boat, 1 sovereign to Mr Staines and 10 shillings each to the coastguards. The *Newry Telegraph*, which had originally reported the story, used the occasion to repeat the need for a Lighthouse at St John's Point: "The captain of the British Heroine has expressed it as his positive conviction that had there been a light on that Point, his vessel would have been saved." (xix) The paper subsequently reported that Lloyd's had made an award of £20 to the crew of the Tyrella Lifeboat "for their meritorious and persevering exertions in saving the crew of the *British Heroine*, driven on shore at Tyrella on 29 November last, while on her passage from Liverpool to Mobile." (xx)

The Tyrella lifeboat is credited with saving the crew of the *Trevor*, en route from Marseilles to Belfast with brimstone [sulphur], when it was driven ashore close to the Coastguard Station on 28 January 1840.

A Royal National Institution silver award for gallantry was made to James Taylor, Tyrella Coastguard, who, in 1845 "took out the lifeboat from the coastguard station to rescue the master and five crew of the *Frolic*" (xxi) which had been driven on shore and totally wrecked.

Although the lifeboat was swamped coming alongside, Taylor continued, with some local fishermen, to rescue the crew from the rigging. The Tyrella lifeboat also featured in newspaper reports of two ships, wrecked within hours of each other in a great storm in 1847:

> During the storm on Friday, two schooners were driven on the Ballyvaston shore near Tyrella, one of which soon became a total wreck. The crew of the *Lowther* were, with great exertions by the Tyrella lifeboat, saved. The ship was laden with coal.' (xxii)

A recommendation for gallantry was made to the Institute by AH Montgomery of Tyrella House (signed as Magistrate and Deputy Lieutenant of the Co Down); in his capacity as a J.P. he was present at the scene to ensure the safety of the ship and cargo (as he was for virtually all wrecks on the eight mile stretch of coastline from St John's Point to Dundrum Bar). He described the bravery of the Lifeboat men in saving the crew of the *Lowther* but added that they:

> …had made every exertion for upwards of two hours at the extreme peril of their own lives to rescue the crew of the schooner *Ida* but were unsuccessful in consequence of the very great storm which was raging at the time. (xxiii)

References to the Tyrella lifeboat become hard to find after 1850, when the *Downpatrick Recorder* noted the rescue of the crew of the barque *Sarah Ann* "in great distress off Tyrella". The lifeboat was manned by the coastguards who, "assisted by four countrymen, made for the relief of the suffering mariners" (xxiv) Like many contemporary newspaper reports, it does not say how many crew were saved, so accurate figures are hard to come by. The first Tyrella lifeboat can only be accurately credited with the 20 sailors rescued from the *British Heroine*, but newspaper accounts credit it with saving the crews of the *Trevor*, the *Lowther*, and the *Sarah Ann*. By the late 1840's, the records of the Institution were less meticulous than they had been and there is no record of when the Tyrella lifeboat ceased to function; it does not feature in any local newspaper reports after 1850, and, other than the reference in Thom's Directory (1851) reporting its condition as Good, there is no further mention of it until an article appeared in a Belfast newspaper in late 1859. This reported on the shipwreck of the Austrian brig, the *Tiky*, which hit the Cow and Calf rocks and beached at Tyrella.

The report concluded with the following:

> As an instance of the inefficiency of the old lifeboats, I may mention that the Tyrella lifeboat, although launched and manned with all dispatch, was of no use. Shortly after she

put off, she was capsized and could not be righted in time to render any assistance, the men on board having a very narrow escape from drowning. (xxv)

It seems odd that the Tyrella lifeboat should make a sudden re-appearance after so many years without any reports of her activity; it is possible that the old boat was launched by the coastguards at Tyrella Watch House, where she had been stationed, as the *Tiky* would have been very close to Ringsallin Point. It is equally possible that the coastguards manned their own six oar galley, which, without any buoyancy aids, would never have been able to withstand high seas and would probably have been swamped. Like all good mysteries, we shall never know.

Chapter 3:
Re-birth

The lack of accurate records held by the Royal National Institution for Preservation of Life from Shipwreck in 1849 was not surprising; by then the organisation:

> …was in a very depressed state, the public having lost all interest in it. Some of the local life-boat associations had ceased to exist and many of the lifeboats had been allowed to fall into decay….the whole system was in such a low state that among all the lifeboats in the United Kingdom, there were perhaps not a dozen really efficient boats. (i)

In hindsight the charity had been flawed from the start, but it was of its time… a coming together of the great and the good with one-off generous donations to fund a worthy cause. Lifeboats and rocket-launchers were built and provided around the coastline of Britain and Ireland, medals were struck and awarded (although with quite a marked class bias), and monetary rewards were given for outstanding bravery by crews and individuals. Many would have said it fulfilled its brief. However, there was no effort to engage the public, other than the occasional newspaper stirrings caused by a disaster or a daring rescue (such as Grace Darling), no effort to widen the base of its donations and no methodical check on the condition or state of repair of its lifeboats.

The crisis in the fortunes of the institution was averted in 1850–1851 by a number of factors which together re-invigorated the charity. By default, on her succession to the throne in 1837, the young Queen Victoria became the Patron of the Institution, but it was a nominal connection only. However, in 1850, the Prince Consort, Prince Albert, who had an interest in all things innovative, agreed to become a Vice-Patron of the Institution; the Queen authorised a donation of £100 and an annual donation of £50 thereafter. Such active royal patronage was very important, and many followed her example; the total income of the charity in 1849 had barely reached £380, so the cash injection was extremely welcome. Money, however, whilst an essential ingredient to the charity, was not its principal problem at that stage.

The institution had become stale and lacked direction; it needed a disciplined and structured approach to the business of preserving life from shipwreck. This crucial element in the turning around of the fortunes of the Institution was provided, firstly, by the young, energetic and very efficient Richard Lewis, Barrister-at-Law, who was appointed in 1850 as its first paid Secretary,

(14) Richard Lewis,
Secretary RNLI
(1850–1883)

the subsequent appointment in 1851 of Algernon, Duke of Northumberland, as its President and in 1852, of Commander JR Ward who was appointed as first Inspector of Lifeboats. The appointments seem to have had a very beneficial effect on Thomas Wilson, the Liberal MP who had been one of the original founding fathers of the charity in 1824. As part of the newly invigorated inner Committee, he represented the most important link with the founding principles but was open to the suggestions for change and renovation that were so clearly necessary. A new triumvirate took over the Institution.

> When the institution was founded in 1824, England was still in the aftermath of the Napoleonic Wars. Increasing trade was certainly beginning to generate wealth, but the country was nothing like as stable or as prosperous as it was 25 years later, in mid-century. The Great Exhibition took place in 1851 when all the world came to admire England's wealth, progress and enlightenment. There was a feeling of confidence in the country. (ii)

It was this feeling of confidence that the Institution needed to tap into, in order to restore the Institution's good name and continue its important work. Richard Lewis set about persuading people to trust the Institution and part with the money needed to fund the initial changes;

personnel began to change and procedures were rapidly set in place:

> Part-time dukes and archbishops were being replaced by full-time naval officers, men who
> brought to the Institution that practical knowledge of seamanship previous lacking... in
> a word, the new men were more professional; and each year, in their first decade of office
> they initiated changes that helped the ailing charity first to survive, then to prosper. (iii)

Lewis established a journal, *The Lifeboat*, in 1852, at the cheapest possible price of 1½d so
all could afford it. It brought tales of stirring rescues, of tragic losses, of medals awarded for
bravery, stories of the recipients who had earned them and information on lifeboats to educate
a growing public able to read and hungry for such stories. Lewis wrote most of the early articles
himself and became very conversant with lifeboat technicalities.

However, one of the most pressing tasks was the design of a new lifeboat, one that would
address the failings of the old Palmer and Plenty boats that were too heavy for launching, difficult
to manoeuvre even in water, and very expensive to build and maintain. Technical advances in the
first half of the century meant that there were better ways to make the boats more buoyant, new
means of assisting the boat to right itself if capsized and ways of allowing water to escape if too
much sea was shipped. As the previous chapter showed, these were all problems endemic to the
early lifeboats. Algernon, Duke of Northumberland donated a prize purse of £100 (worth well
over £10,000 today) for the best design that would address these faults; entries had to include
a scale model as well as the plans of the proposed lifeboat. With such an incentive, it is not
surprising that over 280 entries were received, and a very distinguished judging panel of naval
architects and captains of sea-going vessels as well as the Committee, considered the entries
and finally made their decision. The prize went to a Mr Beeching; however, the committee was
not convinced his was the best possible design and they asked one of the judges, Mr Peake, a
master shipwright at the Royal Dockyard, Woolwich, to use the best features of all the entries to
come up with a better design. The result was the Peake SR (self-righting) Lifeboat, which, with
improvements and modifications over the years, was the staple lifeboat used by the RNLI 'fleet'
for the next 30 years. (See Appendix 4 for information on the Peake design.)

Once the lifeboat design had been satisfactorily sorted, the next priority for the Institution
was to address the issue of its public perception and support. The task of convincing the public
at large to support the charity was obviously a long-term strategy but the 'public' that the
Institution was targeting was different to that of 1824; then it was the wealthy upper classes who
had to be persuaded to support it with philanthropic donations. Now the Institution needed to
attract the educated middle classes, the merchants and professional classes, those with money

(15) A Self-Righting lifeboat and its crew

as well as the social and political standing to positively influence central government's policy on matters maritime.

The problem of how to create a State that would make Society fairer but wouldn't interfere too much in the lives of the individual was the most important question for those who professed themselves Liberals; the struggle to find the right balance occupied politicians for much of the latter part of the 19th/early part of the 20th century. The Institution's Committee in the 1850's, however, was convinced that the State had to take some responsibility for developments in maritime trade and it lobbied hard for change. The Merchant Shipping Act of 1854 was a landmark Act that, like much of the early Health and Safety legislation surrounding mills, mines and factories, was far from perfect, needing years before adequate Inspectors and further legislation made clauses enforceable. It established, however, the right of the State to legislate in favour of the less well off, even if that meant at the expense of the merchant class. In maritime terms, it tightened up regulations of pay and discipline between Master and seamen, increased the powers of the Board of Trade to regulate for shipping and standardised the reporting of wrecks by various authorities such as Coastguards, Excise and Lloyd's agents. These figures were then delivered as an annual report to Parliament. Soon afterwards the Board of Trade, as the representative of Government:

...joined cordially with the National Lifeboat Institution in completely re-organising the means of saving life from shipwreck on the coasts of the United Kingdom, the Institute undertaking the management of the Lifeboat system and the Board of Trade, in conjunction with the coastguard, that of the rocket and mortar apparatus. (v)

This relieved the Institution of the responsibility and cost of providing the rocket launchers for use at a shipwreck, as it had endeavoured to do since 1824.

Raising money was an ever-pressing issue for Lewis. It was clear that the one-off donations of the wealthy were no basis for continued income and the Committee had to consider other means of fundraising. A precedent had been set by the newly founded Shipwrecked Fishermen and Mariners' Royal Benevolent Society which had over 49,500 members on its books, who each paid three shillings a year to provide shelter and aid in the event of shipwreck, a gratuity for dependents or, as noted in the last chapter, in cases such as the four sailors from the *Osceola* left stranded in Belfast when the ship sailed with all their possessions on board. It would not be until the century was closing that the National Lifeboat Institution would begin to appeal to the man and woman in the street, but the importance of appealing to a wider public had now been recognised. Richard Lewis began to introduce the idea of 'sponsoring a Lifeboat' through bequests... sometimes in memory of a departed relative, sometimes in thanks for a life saved from shipwreck.

The need to impress upon the public the risks taken by the lifeboatmen, or by fishermen, to save others led to articles and poems that we might consider overly sentimental today, but were designed to stir the hearts of the reading public:

When the storm sweeps o'er the trackless deep with relentless rage and lashes into ungovernable fury the foaming billows which, under the influence of the frenzied tempest, toss their high heads in wild delirium and dash their spray into fantastic foam over the bold headland and jutting rock; when the ceaseless, sullen, sloughing noise of the angry ocean mixes with the shrilly cadences of the furious winds and is heard by the tenants of every homestead for miles along the iron-bound coast, as they nestle round the cheerful fireside, when in the pitchy darkness of the night, the elements struggle as if in strange duel with each other for mastery and the terrible hurricane strikes the heart of everyone that dwells within the tempestuous circle with awe. When the tremendous forces of nature seem inbound and arrogant, humanity feels its impotence and littleness and its absolute dependence on the great unseen; then there are few men in England and fewer wives and daughters who do not offer up a prayer for the safety of those who have

(16) A lifeboat on
her way.

gone down to the sea in ships and who may be wrestling with the fury of the storm. For there is no danger more appalling than shipwreck; and there is no position on which bravery and heroism are oftener displayed than in contending for life against the anger of the wind and waves. Under such circumstances what can be more consoling to the shipwrecked sailor than the knowledge that the Lifeboat is ready to come to succour him in his great distress. (iv)

In the absence of photographs or television, there was only the power of the pen to construct for the readers a scene that evoked the terrible majesty and sheer power of the storm, forces that man could not control, against which a small lifeboat, manned entirely by volunteers, was prepared to venture forth to save lives. Such articles were the propaganda tools of the Institution; the social commentary of Dickens' novels, the work in the Crimea of Florence Nightingale, the 'Lady with the Lamp' and articles and poems such as that above, all served to stir the consciences of a public for whom the welfare of the 'common' people, soldiers and sailors had not hitherto been of much concern.

Another very astute marketing decision was to end the confusion that had begun to exist between the charity and the newly formed Shipwrecked Mariners' Institution. From 1854 the 'Shipwreck Institution' was no more; the name changed to the National Lifeboat Institution, which became the Royal National Lifeboat Institution in 1860, when Queen Victoria granted it a Royal Charter of Incorporation. (The acronym RNLI was not used until well into the 20th century). The Shipwrecked Mariners' Institution got an assurance from the Lifeboat Institution that it would not use its funds for the upkeep of dependents or in any other way encroach on the new charity's work and in return the Lifeboat Institution got several lifeboats that had been run under the auspices of the Shipwrecked Mariners' institution. Algernon, Duke of Northumberland also handed over to the control of the Lifeboat Institution the previously independent lifeboat stations along the Northumberland coast. The Dublin Ballast Board's lifeboats, which had existed in some cases before the charity was founded in 1824, were also handed over to the control of the Lifeboat Institution in the early 1860's.

Such votes of confidence in the reformed Institution were gratifying but the real boost came with the legacy left in 1856 by Captain Hamilton Fitzgerald RN. He left the enormous sum of £10,000 (over £1,000,000 today) and the decision of the Committee was unanimous – open lifeboat stations around the coastline so that in the event of shipwreck anywhere round the coast of the United Kingdom there would be at least one lifeboat close at hand. Board of Trade statistics for ship losses in UK waters 1852–1871 show an upward trend from a total loss of 5,226 ships from 1852–1856 to a staggering 9,028 lost from 1867–1871. This obviously reflected the increasing number of ships, including many from foreign ports able to trade directly with Britain once the Mercantilist regulations had been lifted. The need for more lifeboats and lifeboat stations was great and the bequest could not have been more opportune. There needed to be many stations because there was a limited range to the lifeboat, powered only by oars and occasionally sail; the area that a Lifeboat could cover was very much restricted to how far and for how long her crew could physically manage her in heavy seas.

Lessons, however, had been learned from the mistakes of the 'Shipwreck Institution'; regulations governing the use and maintenance of lifeboats were pinned up in each RNLI Boat House. Inspectors checked regularly on each Station, and reports were made as to the fitness of the boat, its equipment and its crew.

Coxswains and Assistant Coxswains were paid; they were interviewed for their suitability and appointed by local Committees who reported quarterly to the Institution. In the event that a Branch Committee did not apply regulations properly, the Committee could be summarily dismissed and a new one appointed. The Institution needed to know that once a Station was set up, it would work according to the Regulations and not go its own way, as had happened in the past.

In Ireland, up to 1849 there were, on paper, eleven lifeboat stations, only one of which was in the North… Tyrella, at the Coastguard Station. As we have seen, the lifeboat was inactive after 1852, and so the first Station opened under the auspices of the re-formed National Lifeboat Institution was in 1854, just six miles from Tyrella, at Newcastle, Co Down, on the south-western end of Dundrum Bay. By the end of the 1850's a further thirteen stations had been opened (and three closed) in Ireland, including a second station opened in the North in 1858 at Groomsport on the Ards peninsula, guarding the approaches to Belfast Lough.

In Newcastle, Co Down, Earl Annesley paid for the building of a Boat House in preparation for the first lifeboat, which arrived in 1854. It was 28 ½ feet long and was used to save 5 people but was not the most advanced boat, coming as it did before the newly designed lifeboats came

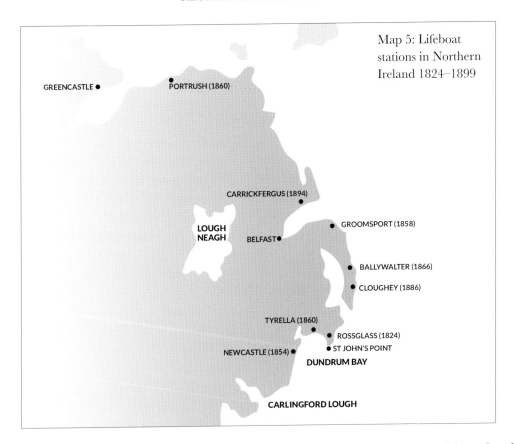

Map 5: Lifeboat stations in Northern Ireland 1824–1899

GREENCASTLE ●

PORTRUSH (1860) ●

CARRICKFERGUS (1894) ●

LOUGH NEAGH

GROOMSPORT (1858) ●

BELFAST ●

BALLYWALTER (1866) ●

CLOUGHEY (1886) ●

TYRELLA (1860) ●

ROSSGLASS (1824) ●

ST JOHN'S POINT ●

NEWCASTLE (1854) ●

DUNDRUM BAY

CARLINGFORD LOUGH

into production. In 1859 the Boathouse was extended to accommodate the new lifeboat that the National Committee had decided to send out, recognising the importance of it to the dangerous Dundrum Bay. The boat was a 30 foot, self-righting Peake, presented by a donor from Reigate and therefore named 'The Reigate'. It was launched 24 times, (1859–1881), and saved 55 people.

Shortly after it arrived in Newcastle, the *Downpatrick Recorder* carried the following article:

> The Royal National Institution wrote to Captain Ridge [Inspecting Commander of Coastguards in Newcastle Division] to inform him that a benevolent Lady had offered to pay for a Lifeboat for the Institution. AH Montgomery is doing his best to secure the boat for Tyrella. (vi)

Chapter 4:
The Tyrella

Arthur Hill Montgomery, was a Montgomery of Greyabbey, one of the oldest Plantation families in Ulster. He had bought Tyrella House and Demesne in 1832 and was a very prominent personage in the area… a JP, Deputy Lieutenant and County Treasurer. He was married to Lady Matilda, one of the daughters of the 5th Earl of Macclesfield, and sister to Lady Amelia, who had married AH Montgomery's older brother, William. After William's untimely death in 1831, the two families became even closer, with Lady Amelia and her only son, Hugh, spending time at Tyrella House, especially during school holidays. Both Lady Amelia and Hugh Montgomery were important contributors to, and life-long supporters of, the Tyrella Lifeboats.

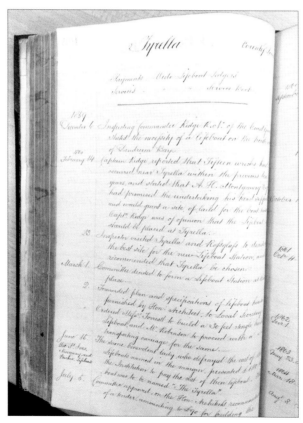

(17) Inspector's report on Tyrella, 1859.

Captain Ridge informed the RNLI that 15 wrecks had occurred in the vicinity of Tyrella between 1850–1860, that there was a real need for a lifeboat station at the north-eastern end of Dundrum Bay, and that AH Montgomery would grant land free for the Boat House site. The RNLI District Inspector visited both Tyrella and Rossglass and agreed with Ridge that the new RNLI station should be at Tyrella. The March minutes indicate the Committee:

> …decided to form a lifeboat station at that place; forwarded plan and specifications of lifeboat house furnished by Hon Architect to Local Secretary; ordered Messrs Forrest to build a 30 foot single bank lifeboat & Mr Robinson to proceed with the transporting carriage for the same. (i)

The tighter controls of the RNLI over its local branches and lifeboat stations was evident in the thoroughness with which the proposed new station at Tyrella was checked, the principal consideration being financial:

> The total cost of a lifeboat establishment would be about £350 – viz for boat and equipment £180; transporting carriage £60; Boat House £110; the Committee want to know how much of this sum would be likely to be raised in the locality. (ii)

The efforts of AH Montgomery to secure the funding necessary to establish a station were successful, and the Tyrella Branch of the Royal National Lifeboat Institution was formed. The purchase of the boat had been paid for as a gift from a Lady who wished to remain anonymous, but who had provided the Institution with £740:

> …to defray the expense of building and equipping four lifeboats… the munificent gift of this lady is a long promised donation, to which she was activated by witnessing a fatal shipwreck in Ireland some years ago and she then resolved to present several lifeboats for exposed parts of the coast. (iii)

The *Freeman's Journal* added that the lady had "requested the Lifeboat might be called *The Tyrella* in honour of AH Montgomery… Indeed the success of the undertaking is mainly to be attributed to and will always remain a monument of his zeal." (iv)

The identity of the benevolent lady remained unreported in every newspaper and RNLI account, with one exception. Reporting on the launch and inauguration of the new lifeboat in September a local paper revealed the lady to be the wife of AH Montgomery… Lady Matilda. (v)

(18) Tyrella Lifeboat House from the South East.   (19) Side elevation from the East.

It was perhaps just a guess; the Boat House was built on land donated by AH Montgomery and the lifeboat was named *The Tyrella* in his honour, by request. Lady Matilda had certainly been a witness to several distressing shipwrecks on the shores of Tyrella, close to her home, and is mentioned in a number of newspaper reports over the years as having helped to look after survivors. Lady Matilda was also a half-sister of Laura, Countess of Antrim, who had personally secured a lifeboat for Portrush in the same year (1860). However, we shall never know, as RNLI records never revealed the Lady's name, only that she had also gifted lifeboats that were sent to St Ives, Newquay and Buckie in Scotland.

On September 15 it was noted that the Boat House had been completed, the boat and carriage were ready, and the harbour trial successfully carried out; the lifeboat was passed fit to be transported to her new station. The launch of *The Tyrella* in September 1860 was a very grand social affair; over 60 of the most important contributors to the Tyrella Branch were invited to watch the launch and to enjoy a splendid luncheon in the Boat House afterwards. The list of attendees read like the Who's Who of south-east County Down: Lord de Ros, Col Forde of Seaforde (MP), JR Allen of Mountpanther, JW Maxwell of Finnebrogue, Hugh Montgomery of Rosemount, Greyabbey, James C Price of Saintfield House, Mr & Mrs Gordon of Delamont, William Keown of Ballydugan House and Aubrey de Vere Beauclerk of Ardglass Castle, being the most prominent of the guests.

Also amongst the guests was Conway Pilson, the Editor of the *Downpatrick Recorder*, which subsequently carried a long account of the events of the day; his descriptions, in the absence of photographs, give a clear picture of the scene:

The site of the Boat House, granted free by AH Montgomery, is about mid-way between St John's Point and Dundrum and nearly opposite the reef of rocks called the Cow and the Calf, and within a gunshot of where the *SS Great Britain* was stranded. [The SS Great Britain had been stranded in Dundrum Bay, for eleven months in 1846/7]. The Boat House is forty feet long and fourteen feet wide – a substantial building of stone with a slated roof. In front of the entrance is a tablet 'TYRELLA LIFEBOAT SUPPORTED BY VOLUNTARY CONTRIBUTION 1860'. Inside the Boat House are suspended RULES FOR THE TREATMENT OF THE DROWNED and THE LIFEBOAT REGULATIONS, with a list of names of the contributors to the fund. The interior was decorated with flowers and evergreens and the walls were covered with flags. (vi)

The Tyrella Boat House had been built to an authorised design, supplied by the central RNLI Committee. After being made redundant in 1899 it was sold back to the landowner, Clarence Craig. Pictures of it now, allow us to imagine what it might have looked like. (See Appendix 5 for information on RNLI Boat Houses and their equipment.)

For all its secular purposes, the building was distinctly ecclesiastical in appearance and very much of its period. A few survive… but such rarities have to be sought out. As a rule, they have disappeared. (vii)

The launch began at one o'clock, when the boat was drawn on its carriage down to the water's edge by four horses. A salute of six guns was sounded as the boat was launched off its carriage, with a crew of eight, under the command of David Kirk, Chief Boatman of the Tyrella Coastguard Station, who was acting coxswain on the day. The oarsmen pulled out beyond the rocks called the Cow and the Calf, then one of the crew (a Coastguard called Adam Murphy, who shortly afterwards became the new coxswain of the Tyrella lifeboat) jumped overboard to demonstrate the usefulness of the life-belt; he swam about and then floated until picked up by the lifeboat. (The life-belt was a vest made up of strips of cork sewn into canvas pockets and shaped to tie round the middle; designed by Commander Ward, it had proved itself reliable as a life preserver since 1854 and was mandatory apparel for all lifeboat crews.) The boat sent by the RNLI was of the Peake design; it was 30 feet long, 7 feet wide and rowed by 8 oars. It had the key features of self-righting if capsized and the ability to eject water if swamped.

By an ingenious contrivance the boat, with her crew on board, is launched on the carriage. With their oars in their hands, they are enabled to obtain headway before the breakers

(20) Lifeboat being moved by team of four horses in Newcastle, Co Down.

have time to beat the boat broadside on the beach. The hauling up of the lifeboat on her carriage is accomplished with equal facility. (viii)

Less than one month after *The Tyrella* arrived on station she had her first 'shout':

During the past week the prevailing wind has been from the south-west and on the night of Wednesday 17 instant, the wind rose high and blew in strong gusts from the same quarter. Dundrum Bay is always dangerous during the prevalence of a gale from southward. Between the hours of eleven and twelve o'clock, a vessel bearing lights was observed by the Tyrella Coastguard in that Bay, driving before the gale and in great danger of being stranded on a projecting reef of rocks jutting out from the Coastguard Station. No time was lost. Blue lights were burned, and rockets sent up both from the Station and from Flagstaff Hill at Tyrella House, warning the vessel of her dangerous nearness to the shore… Captain Ridge, the humane and indefatigable superintendent of the Coastguard Stations of this District, who was on duty at the spot at the time, recommended the immediate calling into requisition of the Tyrella lifeboat. Within a very short time this recommendation was carried into effect.

Though the night was extremely dark and thick with drenching rain, and the greater part of the men in attendance on the boat were scattered in the outlying cottages, they were quickly collected. Horses, under the kind permission of AH Montgomery Esq. were procured from Tyrella stables and the lifeboat on its ponderous carriage was transported over anything but smooth and easy roads in a thick darkness from Tyrella to St John's Point, a distance of some five miles in little more than an hour. The distressed ship, which turned out to be the *Martha Whitmore*, 700 tons burthen, bound from Richmond, Virginia to Glasgow with a cargo of wheat and flour, warned of her danger at Tyrella, wore off before the wind with the intention no doubt of clearing the Bay, but unfortunately, either from ignorance of her position or some other cause, she was unable to do so and ran aground almost close to the Lighthouse at St John's Point.

No immediate danger, however, was apprehended and the crew remained on board, although the captain was taken ashore in the St John's boat, as the tide had nearly ebbed from the ship. The services of the Tyrella boat, on its arrival, were not actually needed; yet the greatest credit is due to the men to whose charge it was committed for the promptitude with which, under the most unfavourable circumstances, it was conveyed to the place where it might have been requisite.

The stranding of a vessel in the Bay so soon after the establishment of the Tyrella Lifeboat – for it is not a month since an account of its launch and inauguration appeared in our columns – is a proof of the urgent need of the presence of such a ready succour, in times of peril in so dangerous a locality as the Bay of Dundrum; and the willingness and readiness of the crew and men connected with the service of the boat, so soon after the embodiment, and on this, their first assay of active service, entered upon their arduous task, is an augury of their effectual and cordial co-operation at any future time when their services might be required. We accord them the highest praise for their conduct on this occasion, and at the same time cannot but express our sense of the zeal and energy of Captain Ridge in directing their efforts and organising their movements. We have the highest hopes of the Tyrella boat, with so willing a crew and under such able superintendence. (ix)

The newspaper account, although somewhat wordy, gives us a picture of the dreadful weather conditions under which the men had to work, and it also serves to illustrate some of the key features of the lifeboats of the time:

It is also necessary that the lifeboat is supplied with means of transportation on the land, for wrecks might occur at a distance of several miles from the spot where she is stationed, yet close to the shore. In such cases, it is usually much safer and more expeditious for the Lifeboat to be conveyed by land to that part of the shore contiguous to the wreck than for her to be rowed or sailed, broadside to the sea, through perhaps miles of broken water. (x)

Modern means of communication not being available in 1860, the crew and launchers had to be individually contacted and assembled, and, in the event of a launch at night or in poor weather, the whole illuminated by storm lanterns or oil lamps. There were no street lights, no tarmacadam or concrete roads, just dirt tracks which, in bad weather, would have been mud baths. Horsing a four ton lifeboat over such roads in drenching rain for a distance of more than five miles in just over an hour, was an achievement of which to be proud, although it must have seemed anti-climactic to the men of Tyrella on this, their first rescue.

Mandatory practices for the lifeboat and its crew were part of the tighter regulations that the Lifeboat Institution had set in place. Held once a quarter, unless the lifeboat had been on active service that quarter, they were designed to ensure the crew knew how to handle the boat in all conditions, new recruits could be familiarised with lifeboat routine and any defects noted and dealt with. The first practice of the Tyrella lifeboat was held at the end of January 1861:

> Wednesday last, the weather being very tempestuous in Dundrum Bay and the seas running very high, a trial was made of the Tyrella lifeboat and of all the expertness of her crew, in order to test the value of the services they would be able to render for the saving of life in the event of a shipwreck occurring. About one o'clock the boat was brought out and the crew, under the direction of Captain Ridge RN (Inspecting Officer of Coastguards, Newcastle Division) were exercised for an hour in that portion of the Bay where wrecks most frequently occur and made to go through manoeuvres in the water as if a vessel were in distress on the rocks, on a plan somewhat analogous to that in which the discipline of a body of troops is tried on a field in a sham fight. The boat was pulled in a heavy sea and through a terrible surf onto the point at which a vessel would be stranded, several times returning to the shore and going back again to the supposed wreck, in the course of which operations she was four times almost completely filled with water by the waves dashing over her, but each time she almost immediately righted. The trial was sufficient to satisfy all who saw it as to the efficiency of the boat and crew and of the essential aid they could give whenever their services might be unhappily called into requisition. (xi)

Lifeboat Regulations were quite explicit about what a lifeboat and its crew could do on coming up to a wreck; their principal job was the saving of life and they were not to be used as a means of salvage, or to take orders to a ship from those on shore, or to take on or off pilots, without explicit permission. These regulations were tested in the next 'shout' for *The Tyrella* in June 1861. A short local newspaper article indicated a second fruitless call out for the boat:

> The *John Bull* was driven into Dundrum Bay in dense fog by a south-easterly gale. The boat succeeded in anchoring a short distance between St John's Point and Ballyvaston. The Tyrella lifeboat went out but was not needed. (xii)

However, about a month later, at a meeting of the Belfast Harbour Commissioners, a damning indictment made of the crew of the Tyrella lifeboat was widely reported in local and regional papers:

> Mr Boyd, agent at Lloyd's stated that the crew of the lifeboat at Tyrella refused to put out

to the vessel's assistance [*John Bull*] without the permission of the Inspecting Commander who lived in Newcastle. The crew said it would be as much as their situation was worth to put out without the Commander's permission. Mr Boyd called the Agent of the Lifeboat Association to the matter and stated that, on the day in question, the weather was not so violent as to prevent him (and his son) from going out to the ship in a small boat. (xiii)

Some ten days letter, correspondence from Captain Ridge appeared in the papers, setting out what had really happened:

In your paper of the 17th inst, I observed that a statement was made at a meeting of the Belfast Harbour Commissioners. As I was, at that time, Inspecting Commander of Newcastle Division, I consider it an act of justice to the crew of the Tyrella lifeboat to send you the particulars of the case referred to, as they came to my immediate notice. The barque, *John Bull* of Liverpool, got embayed in Dundrum Bay on the afternoon of the 11th June last, and being unable to clear St John's Point, she brought up her anchors about five miles from the Lifeboat's station at Tyrella.

The Lifeboat (without any unnecessary delay and without waiting for any communication from the Inspecting Commander) was taken round on her carriage to the nearest point to the ship. She was launched about 11.00pm and boarded the vessel at about 1.30 in the morning of the 12th. The coxswain ascertained from the master of the vessel that he did not require the services of the Lifeboat – neither did he require any assistance whatsoever. The coxswain also arranged with the master that in the event of the services of the lifeboat being afterwards required, the vessel would make a signal of distress by showing her colours if in the day and by lights if at night.

The Lifeboat returned to the shore at daylight, she was placed again on her carriage ready for launching; the weather having moderated considerably, the crew were ordered by me to return to their station, with the perfect understanding that they were to proceed to the vessel without delay in the event of her requiring the Lifeboat. The vessel did not make any signal of distress, neither was she in any greater danger than when the master declined assistance. The services of the boat and crew were not afterwards required. A Lifeboat being solely for the purpose of saving life, they are not allowed, by the regulations of the Institution, to take orders off to a ship, nor to interfere with any private enterprise, without the special permission of the local Committee. (xiv)

We can only surmise what occasioned the last sentence of the statement, but it seems very probable that Mr Boyd, as an agent of Lloyd's, was desirous of communicating with the ship, either to give orders about the cargo or suggest a course of action, and the lifeboat coxswain very properly refused to do so without express permission from the Committee or the Inspecting Commander. It is obvious that Mr Boyd went out to the ship on the 12th, when the weather had moderated, in order to pass on his message personally, but it is less obvious what he hoped to gain from his comment at the Belfast Harbour Commissioners. At best, he did not know of the Regulations and thought the coxswain very unaccommodating, a matter which he may have felt needed to be reported; in any event he was publicly shaming a coxswain and volunteer crew, a matter which Captain Ridge's letter soon cleared up.

The first rescue attributed to the Tyrella lifeboat came a full year after it was stationed and merited only the shortest mention in local papers and in *Lloyd's List*. The newspaper reports simply stated that the schooner *Glasgow*, from Wick to Waterford with a cargo of herring had been driven ashore in Dundrum Bay, the cargo had been safely discharged and the crew rescued by the Tyrella lifeboat; there was no indication of the number of crew saved. The next 'shout' was to the *Solferino*, (89 tons registered, from Balbriggan to Ardrossan in ballast) which was driven ashore at Rathmullen on 11 January 1862; despite remaining on station all night, the assistance of the Lifeboat was not required, and she returned at daybreak to the Boat House. The reference to remaining on station all night, used in many press articles, glosses over the hardship involved for the lifeboat crew, as an 1894 text explained:

> …what it means is that they decided to remain the whole of a long winter's night in freezing storm and tempest, buffeted, drenched, exposed to all the murderous fury of a terrible storm… It is easy to picture what terrible risks, not only to health but to life, these lion-hearted men must often run by spending a deadly winter's night on a stormy sea in order to save life or indeed on the merest chance of saving life. (xv)

However, less than a week later, the schooner *Bellona* of Belfast, bound from Liverpool to the quayside at Dundrum with coal, had been driven onto the sands at the eastern edge of Dundrum Bar, becoming a total wreck. Four of the crew were driven to the rigging, but the force of the winds and the heavy seas swept them to their deaths. The master alone had managed to cling on, but his plight was not noticed until daylight, when he was spotted from the shore by a local fisherman. Mr Felix Redmond and his three brothers, with two coastguards, set off in Redmond's fishing boat to rescue him; the seas were so high that the boat was almost instantly swamped and capsized, throwing the six men into the water. Fortunately, they were able to cling

(21) Service book of *The Tyrella*.

to the keel of the upturned boat and were rescued by the manager of the Marquis of Downshire's estate, James Cunningham, in one of his Lordship's own boats.

> …it was in vain, however, on account of the lightness of the Marquis' pleasure boat, to attempt to reach the wreck to which the captain was still clinging with the grasp of death, the sea breaking over him with fearful violence. However, just as hope seemed to desert him, the Tyrella lifeboat, as beautiful a craft as ever breasted the storms of ocean, hove in sight and nearing the wreck, rescued the poor Captain from his perilous position. The Newcastle boat shortly followed, but its services were not required, as the other was already, like a thing of life and beauty, bidding defiance to wind and waves, on its way to land with the sufferer. (xvi)

The National Lifeboat Institution had tweaked the 'Shipwreck Institution's' tradition of making monetary rewards for bravery at a rescue; every call-out or shout was now rewarded, in proportion to the time spent on call, in order to recompense the volunteers for time lost from their ordinary jobs. The Hon Secretary of the Tyrella Branch (AH Montgomery, who held the post from 1860 to his death in 1867) had the following notice inserted in local papers in February 1862:

> The Hon Secretary of the Tyrella Branch of the Royal National Lifeboat Institution acknowledges to have received from the Committee of this valuable Institution, the following sums for services rendered by the Tyrella lifeboat to vessels wrecked and in distress, as underneath:
>
> | | | |
> |---|---|---|
> | October 18 1860 | The *Martha Whitmore*, stranded at St John's Point | £4.12.00 |
> | June 12 1861 | The *John Bull*, in distress off Rossglass | £7.02.00 |
> | September 27 1861 | The *Glasgow*, wrecked off Rossglass | £3.14.00 |
> | January 11 1862 | The *Solferino*, wrecked on Rathmullan Point | £5.12.06 |
> | January 17 1862 | The *Bellona*, wrecked near Dundrum Bar | £6.10.00 (xvii) |

There are no records in RNLI Archives, newspapers or *Lloyd's List* for any rescue launches of the Tyrella lifeboat in 1863. In January 1864 it was called out to the barque *Hamilton Gray*, which had got into difficulties on the southern end of Dundrum Bay. The Newcastle lifeboat, the *Reigate*, had taken off some of the crew but had been damaged in doing so, and the assistance of *The Tyrella* was requested. However, when she got to the wreck, the crew had managed to launch their own boat and make their way to shore; *The Tyrella* stayed on station to check for survivors, and when all was clear, made its way back to the Boat House. There were two other launches in 1864 but in the end the services of the lifeboat were not required at either.

> It may be stated that launches of lifeboats, unattended with positive results have been during the year unusually frequent. But such occasions are not times for hesitation. Those who are wise after the fact are not in a position to judge of the reasons which at such times influence lifeboat crews, who, seeing a vessel with a distress signal or in a perilous position, falter not between two opinions but proceed out at once to offer help. Which as it often happens, she may not from various subsequent causes ultimately need. The lifeboat-men cannot say until they reach her that the vessel is not in distress and hesitation at such critical periods may mean the loss of valuable lives. (xviii)

The last reported launch of The Tyrella came in December 1865, when the schooner, *Daniel O'Connell*, (from Liverpool to Newry with a cargo of Indian corn) was driven ashore at Rathmullen, and:

> …was in danger of being smashed to pieces by the fury of the gale which was blowing from the south-east and by the returning ebb-tide…the schooner's crew were in great danger of being washed overboard by the great breakers which lashed in foam over the deck. The lifeboat was launched at half-past one, abreast of the schooner after having been brought there on the carriage, driven by the horses of AH Montgomery Esq. Too much praise cannot be given to the crew who exerted themselves nobly and well and had the satisfaction of landing the whole of the schooner's crew – five in number – safely on the shore, amid the deafening applause of scores of the neighbouring peasantry. (xix)

The Institution's Lifeboat Regulations stipulated that each station's local Committee, carry out specified duties, such as employing the coxswain and assistant coxswain, and holding a quarterly meeting to sign–off their report to the Institution. This covered matters such as 'shouts', exercises, any matters of discipline dealt with or outstanding and reporting defects or problems with equipment. This was to ensure that the national body had an oversight of everything that was going on locally and therefore a good picture of how the Institution was performing nationally. However, lifeboats, like everything else, wear out and have to be replaced by new ones. In such cases, framed metal tablets are put up in the Boat Houses, recording fully the services of the previous lifeboat on the station. (xx)

Unfortunately, no Service Boards for the Tyrella station can be traced. The Inspecting Officer of Lifeboats carried out annual routine inspections of the Tyrella station from 1861 to 1865, reporting things to be in excellent order. However, in October 1866 the Assistant Inspector, found the port side of the lifeboat quite rotten and recommended a new boat and carriage. (xxi)

Chapter 5:
Change and Controversy

There was much less fanfare made about the arrival of the second lifeboat at Tyrella. A short press article on 22 December 1866 noted:

> Its excellent formation and complete arrangements as a vessel for saving life was the source of much admiration. The workmanship is of a very superior description and everything about it is executed in a substantial manner. Its name, *The Tyrella*, is painted in gold letters on the bow. (i)

Sadly, AH Montgomery, who had worked tirelessly to secure and then support the first Lifeboat, died early in 1867 after a very short illness and never got to see the second Lifeboat in action.

The new lifeboat was only in place a few months and had just finished her first trial, when a French fishing sloop, *William of Paimpol*, carrying salt and provisions for cod fishing off Iceland, came ashore 1 mile from the Tyrella Coastguard Station.

> The crew laid out both anchors in the hopes of getting her off as she was stranded at low water mark and the crew could have walked off but chose not to do so. As the gale increased and the tide made, it was known that the ship would probably part from her anchors or founder in the broken water – and, indeed, she shortly did so. The lifeboat of the National Lifeboat Institution was quickly launched and proceeded to the scene of the wreck; in the meantime, seven of the crew had left in their own boat and had succeeded in reaching the shore but were unable to return for the remainder of their crew. The vessel soon foundered, and the sea washed completely over her. When near the wreck, two of the oars of the lifeboat were broken and she was driven to leeward and on to the beach, in spite of all the exertions of the crew. The boat was, however, taken to windward and launched, but with a similar lack of success. By this time, through the severity of the weather, some of the gallant men in the lifeboat were exhausted by their exertions, but volunteers were obtained in their place and the boat was again launched and proceeded through the broken water. Every sea filled her, but she behaved most nobly under these

trying circumstances. After great difficulty the vessel was reached and the six poor fellows who were left in her, were rescued from their perilous position and brought safely ashore in the lifeboat. The master fell into the water while endeavouring to reach the boat but was rescued by the exertions of those in her, after being some minutes under water. Great praise is due to the coxswain and crew of the lifeboat for their persevering and gallant services on this occasion as they suffered much from their exertions and exposure to the severe gale then blowing. (ii)

For most readers today, it is a near impossibility to imagine the sheer physical strength, never mind the courage, required to row a 30 foot open boat through mountainous seas, for over three hours, even if most of the crew were fishermen or coastguards and used to the hardships of such a life. It was just as hard for the Victorian middle and upper classes, who lived in their bubble of comfort and respectability; yet it was to these people that Richard Lewis was trying to appeal, to get the funding necessary to further the work of the Institution. The propaganda tools available to him were *The Lifeboat* and newspaper reports, but he was prevailed upon to write a *History of the Lifeboat* in 1874 to address questions and technical details about lifeboats for which there had been many requests. He also used the book to convey to the public, in language which he hoped they would understand, just how courageous the lifeboatmen were:

The dangers to which the crew of a lifeboat are exposed entitle those who encounter them to the greatest credit. It is impossible to exaggerate the awful circumstances attending a shipwreck. Let us picture the time when, after a peaceful sunset and the toils of the day are over, the hero of the lifeboat has retired to rest, and the silence of the night is unbroken, except by the murmur of the winds and the noise of the sea breaking on the shore. With the approach of the storm, however, the wind and waves rise in fury upon the deep and with their mingled vengeance lash the cliffs and the beach. A signal of distress rouses the coxswain and his men, crowds rush in curiosity to the cliffs or line the shore, heedless of the driving rain or the blinding sleet. Barrels of tar are lighted on the coast and the signal gun and the fiery rocket make a fresh appeal to the brave. The Boat House is unlocked and the Lifeboat, with her crew, is dragged hurriedly to the shore. The storm rages wildly and the mountains of surf and sea appal the stoutest heart. The gallant men look dubiously at the work before them and fathers, mothers, wives and children implore them to desist from a hopeless enterprise. The voice of the coxswain prevails however.

(23) Ready to launch.

The lifeboat is launched among the breakers, cutting bravely through the foaming mass – now buried under the swelling billows, or rising on their summit – now dashed against the hapless wreck, still instinct with life – now driven from it by a mountainous wave – now embarking its living freight and carrying them through storm and danger and darkness to a blessed shore. Would that this were the invariable issue of a lifeboat service. The boat that adventures to a disaster meets with disaster itself occasionally, for in the war of elements ere now, the lifeboat crews themselves have been the first victims…. (iii)

None of the Tyrella lifeboats suffered the loss of boat or crew during the whole period of the station's existence, but the Ballywalter lifeboat in Co Down, which had arrived on station in 1866, had an unfortunate incident in December 1868, with tragic consequences:

…suddenly, and before the crew had time to make the slightest effort to prevent the occurrence, a heavy squall struck the boat and capsized her, turning her over completely, with her sails and masts under the water and her bottom uppermost. Robert Boyd, the first cox and George Adair jumped into the sea clear of her; three of the crew: Johnston, Mackenzie and McDowell – held to the seats underneath and the remaining seven hung on to stirrup ropes on the outside of the gunwales on the windward side. The three men hanging onto the seats under the vessel gave themselves up as lost, thinking that, with the three sails and the masts below the water, she could never right herself; but not withstanding these obstacles and the weight of seven men clinging to the outside, she was not more than 30 seconds in this position, when she came right round on an even keel, bringing with her the three men who still were by the seats and these were able to assist all the others on board, except the first cox, Robert Boyd who had drifted a long distance to leeward. He was seen by his mates, struggling in the water, with his head under the cork jacket, which he had neglected to have properly adjusted on leaving the Boat House… the crew, having witnessed trials of the vessel's self-righting properties and seen the enormous leverage power required to upset her, believed that she could live in any sea, and were therefore more lax in their attention to the precautionary instructions laid down for their guidance than they otherwise would have been. (iv)

Robert Boyd was tragically drowned; it is deeply ironic that as coxswain he had particular responsibilities regarding the safety of his crew:

(24) Lifeboatman
with lifebelt.

THE LIFE-BELTS IN USE BY THE CREWS OF THE LIFE-BOATS OF
THE INSTITUTION.

The requisite qualities of a life-boatman's life-belt are—

1. Sufficient extra-buoyancy to support a man heavily clothed, with his head and shoulders above the water, or to enable him to support another person besides himself.

2. Perfect flexibility, so as readily to conform to the shape of the wearer.

3. A division into two zones, an upper and lower, so that between the two it may be secured tightly round the waist; for in no other manner can it be confined sufficiently close and secure round the body without such pressure over the chest and ribs as to materially affect the free action of the lungs, impede the muscular movement of the chest and arms, and thereby diminish the power of endurance of fatigue, which, in rowing boats, is a matter of vital importance.

4. Strength, durability, and non-liability to injury.

The cork life-belts of the NATIONAL LIFE-BOAT INSTITUTION possess the first two qualities in a greater degree than any other life-belt, and the third one exclusively.

In addition to these belts a very full equipment of stores is supplied to the Life-boats of the Institution—such as anchors and cables, grapnels and lines, life-buoys, lanterns, rockets, and many other articles, together with portable or launching-skids.

It is of great importance that the lifeboatman should tie his lifebelt securely around him, since its efficiency and as a consequence, his own life, may depend on its being so. The coxswains of the lifeboat are therefore instructed to be most careful in seeing that on every occasion of going afloat in the lifeboat that each of her crew has his belt properly and securely tied before getting into the boat. (v)

Whether or not Boyd had checked the crew and overlooked his own belt, the accident was a terrible reminder of the importance of meticulously observing the rules. The Ballywalter boat went on to save 142 people in the years 1866–1885, with no further loss of life to crew.

Lifeboat Regulations were stringent, but they had been drawn up by men with experience. Rule 3 of the Regulations was that crews were to be made up of volunteer fishermen and boatmen resident in the district, while Rule 12 acknowledged that there were occasions when gaps in a crew could be filled by the coxswain from volunteers willing to take their place. That had happened with the rescue of the crew from the *William of Paimpol*; there was never a shortage of volunteer crew for the Tyrella lifeboat, and fresh arms pulling on oars after many hours battling waves were sometimes necessary to effect a rescue. Payment was 10 shillings for volunteering by day, and £1 by night; intended to recompense men for time lost, it ensured that there were always plenty of volunteers if regular crew were unavailable.

Barely a month after the rescue of the *William of Paimpol*, the Tyrella lifeboat was at sea again, but her services were not, in the end required:

> …the barque *Charlotte Harrison*, from Liverpool to British North America, was observed from the Tyrella Coastguard Station running towards shore, it being thick fog and blowing a gale from the South. The land was observed by the master and the barque was hauled to the wind and stood for St John's Point but could not weather the Point. After standing towards Dundrum Bay, the master tried again for the Point, with no better success. Seeing that he was close to a lee shore, he let go both anchors and brought the vessel up, about a half mile from Tyrella Watch House, inside the Cow and Calf rocks and close to the Pladdy rocks where a heavy sea was raging. Mr Boyd, seeing the dangerous position of the barque, launched the Tyrella lifeboat and soon reached the ship, but her services were not required. The gale moderated during the night, but the lifeboat was kept on the beach in case the vessel parted her cables. This morning, the barque was taken in tow by a steamer. (vi)

Records show no 'shouts' for the Tyrella lifeboat from April 1867 until February 1870, when, in a heavy gale, the brigantine *Eliza* of Liverpool signalled for assistance. In the end the services of the lifeboat were not required. Sadly, this gap did not mean that there were no shipwrecks in that period in Dundrum Bay, merely that the vessels that did need assistance were south-west of Dundrum Bar and were successfully handled by the Newcastle lifeboat, *The Reigate*. The Assistant Inspector visited the Tyrella station on June 22, 1868 and took the lifeboat out in a fresh breeze and moderate sea. He found things in good order but noted that: "the launchers of the boat were dissatisfied with the usual pay and threatened not to assist in launching" (vii) Lifeboats were cumbersome and heavy and needed the assistance of launchers… men and sometimes women, to help get the lifeboat off its carriage into the sea, or to haul it back up when the service had finished. Launchers were paid 4 shillings per launch; a few launchers went on to become regular crew members, notably William Kerr, who served for 16 years as the Assistant Coxswain of the Tyrella lifeboat, but who began as a launcher when the Tyrella station first opened.

Nothing further was mentioned about the issue of pay for the launchers in subsequent reports for 1869 and 1870 which found everything in 'good order'. Such unannounced visits and quarterly practices kept the crews ready, for when they might be needed.

The next 'shout' came in January 1871, in the middle of one of the worst storms ever remembered:

(25) Launchers bringing in the boat.

> The tempest that has just subsided was accompanied by a deluge of rain and hail, and at
> intervals by vivid lightning and peals of thunder. An immense amount of damage has
> been sustained, the gale having been unparalleled for intensity during the last twenty
> years. (viii)

In the middle of this gale, the barque *Colima*, from Liverpool to Guatemala, was badly
damaged and driven on shore near to the bar at Dundrum. The Tyrella lifeboat went twice to
her assistance, according to contemporary sources, before she grounded. The crew were saved.
However, the incident was unfortunately not without loss of life:

> A man named James Carr was engaged in a flat-bottomed boat or "lighter" with some others,
> in bringing casks from the ship *Colima*, which lies wrecked on the bar of Dundrum. When
> the boat was in close to the harbour, Carr lost his footing and fell overboard… the body was
> found next morning, some distance from the place where he fell into the water. (ix)

In March 1871 fierce gales lashed the eastern coast of Ireland and the Tyrella lifeboat was
called out twice within a week. The first 'shout' was to a brigantine, the *William*, which eventually
grounded at Minerstown. Contemporary newspaper accounts differ in what happened to the
crew; one paper claimed the five crew were taken off by lifeboat, whilst another report had them

rescued by locals. Shortly after this the schooner *Isabella* had a lucky escape when she stranded on the soft sands at Tyrella in March 1871. Although the lifeboat was in attendance, the crew were able to disembark at low tide and the ship stayed stable enough to be towed off by steamer a week later.

The regular inspections of stations and boats ensured problems could be resolved before they became major issues. An interesting insight into Tyrella station was noted in two reports in 1871. In the first, Colonel Sir Fitzroy Clayton, (later Chairman of the RNLI) visited the station on October 24 and found "lifeboat, carriage and House were in excellent order. The compass was deficient, and the coxswain said he would like to have masts and sails for the use of the boat…" Just six weeks later the Assistant Inspector visited the station and took the lifeboat afloat during fine weather. He noted that: "some of the best of the crew had emigrated since his first visit and their places had been supplied by others who were not such good boatmen, although plucky and willing…" He expressed concerns about the coxswain's request for sails as more crew experience would be needed to be able to successfully manage the Tyrella lifeboat. At this visit the District Inspector also noted: "Hon Secretary concerned subscriptions had dropped but he was doing his best to make the station self-sustaining." (x)

The concern about crew emigrating was repeated in 1873, when, after a visit to the station in January where everything was: 'in capital order', the Assistant Inspector took the lifeboat afloat but found the crew rather indifferent. Some of the former crew had emigrated and their places had been filled by farm labourers.

> The 2nd Assistant Inspector thought it very desirable that the services of some of the Coastguard men should be secured to man the boat, and he communicated with the Inspecting Commander on the subject. (xi)

Securing a more participatory role for the Tyrella Coastguard with the Tyrella lifeboat was to prove very important for the success of future rescues.

It was over a year later before *The Tyrella* was next called out, this time to a Norwegian barque, the *Neptunus*, from Liverpool to Copenhagen in ballast, which was driven ashore in a SSE gale close to Tyrella Coastguard Station. *The Lifeboat* carried the story as one of its articles:

> Excellent service was performed by the lifeboat on this station in August 1872; about two o'clock in the morning of that day, during a very heavy gale with a rough sea, the barque *Neptunus* of Soon, Norway, drove ashore in Dundrum Bay. Her crew had previously been compelled to cut away two of the masts to prevent the vessel from being capsized. The

(26) Pounding surf, Tyrella.

> Tyrella lifeboat was got out and with much difficulty was launched through heavy surf. She then proceeded to the wreck and was enabled to save the whole of the shipwrecked crew – some fourteen in number. The lifeboatmen were reported to have behaved with great spirit and gallantry on the occasion. (xii)

The rescue earned the first national recognition for the new RNLI Tyrella lifeboat station, as reported in the local press:

> Voted the Thanks of the Institution, inscribed on vellum, to Mr John Williams, Chief Boatman of H.M. Coastguard at Tyrella and £14 and 9 shillings to the crew of the Tyrella lifeboat for going off during a SSE gale and rescuing 14 persons from the barque *Neptunus*, which was stranded at Tyrella Coastguard Station on 16 August 1872. (xiii)

Since neither the coxswain Adam Murphy or John Gordon, the assistant coxswain were mentioned, it can only be inferred that both were unavailable and that John Williams, as the most experienced of the remaining crew took the boat out. Williams, as Chief Boatman of Tyrella Coastguard Station could not be a permanent coxswain, as it might have interfered with his duties; Adam Murphy was also a coastguard, but he did not have major station responsibilities, in line with Rule 3 of the Lifeboat Regulations which permitted Coastguards to be volunteer crew (with permission from the Admiralty). The Inspector General of Coastguards in Ireland, had, up to his retirement in 1855, been very supportive of Coastguards forming part of a lifeboat crew, and this had continued after Dombrain retired when the Coastguards in Ireland had come under Admiralty control. There was a particularly close relationship between the Lifeboat Station and the Coastguards at Tyrella. The first Tyrella lifeboat had been stationed at the Watch House from 1838–1852 and had been manned and run by the Coastguards themselves, while the RNLI Tyrella Boat House was about ½ mile from the Coastguard Station. From 1821, the Coastguards at Tyrella, whilst operating out of the Watch House, had been living in outlying rented accommodation (as was the normal practice at that time). In 1865, a row of seven terraced cottages was built adjacent to the Watch House, making the Tyrella Station much more self-contained. It made it easier for some Coastguards to man the Lifeboat when needed without reducing the efficiency of the Station. RNLI minutes also noted in July 1875 that:

> The present Inspecting Commander of Coastguards of this Division was a son of the late Admiral Washington and took much interest in the lifeboat cause and the men were more disposed than ever to man the lifeboat which was a great gain as the number of available civilians was diminishing. (xiv)

As well as forming part of the lifeboat crew, the Coastguard kept a look out from their Watch

(27) Tyrella Coastguard Station.

House at Ringsallin Point and alerted the Tyrella coxswain when the lifeboat was required; and so from quite early on, this relationship between the Coastguards and the Lifeboatmen mirrored what it is today… the Coastguard kept watch out to sea, warned ships off that were straying too close to dangerous rocks or hidden reefs and notified the Lifeboat Service if they thought any ship might be in distress or need their assistance. Ultimately the major difference is and was that the Coastguard are government employees (albeit in the 19th century under Admiralty control) whereas the Royal National Lifeboat Institution was and is a charity, independent of government control, although working closely alongside it.

The next rescue for *The Tyrella*, some two years after the *Neptunus*, not only resulted in awards for gallantry to two lifeboat men, but also to a fairly ferocious 'war of words' that raged for many weeks in the columns of the local weekly newspaper. It all began with an account of a shipwreck published in the *Downpatrick Recorder* on 5 December 1874:

> On Saturday night, a brig, the *Donna Maria* of Belfast… from Liverpool to Belfast with greenheart timber for Messrs Harland and Wolff, the eminent ship-builders of that town, was driven ashore during a violent gale from the sea at Ballyvaston. The Tyrella lifeboat was promptly got into readiness, horsed by David McCutcheon, who was himself in attendance and greatly encouraged the men, and reached the scene of the wreck at 10.00pm. With much difficulty and danger five of the crew were got into the lifeboat, and safely brought ashore. One of these, a man of colour, had been injured by the rolling of the heavy timber and fell into the boiling sea. James Toland, coastguard, quickly caught him up and supported him until he was helped into the boat by Hugh Murphy, one of the crew. A sixth man still lay on the deck in a painful condition, one of his legs being caught under one of the timber logs, weighing between 5–6 tons each. Some of the men returned to the vessel when light began to come and John Gordon, vice coxswain, had himself tied outside the ship in mid-air, sawed away a part of the bulwarks, then drove in wedges under the log and so freed the sufferer. He and the 'darky' were at once sent to the Downpatrick infirmary. Too much praise cannot be given to those men who acted as crew on this occasion and we heartily recommend them to the special notice of the Lifeboat Institution and we return grateful thanks to the Divine Provider for the lives saved from this wreck. (xv)

On the face of it this was a story of quite exceptional gallantry, from the saving of the man's life who fell in the sea by James Foland (who went on to become the longest serving coxswain of the Newcastle lifeboat after his retirement from the Coastguards) and the extra-ordinary bravery of the assistant coxswain John Gordon (the Tyrella blacksmith). However, it obviously displeased at least one person. A very long letter appeared in the columns of the *Downpatrick Recorder* the following Saturday:

Dear Sir, I, with many of your readers, was struck with amazement at a paragraph which appeared in your issue of last Saturday, relative to the wreck at Ballyvaston, of the brigantine *Donna Maria*…"a sixth man still lay on the deck in a painful condition under one of the timber logs…" I thought it most unaccountable, that men just themselves saved from a watery grave, should have been so inhumane and have so far forgotten what they owed to a suffering brother as to have left him in such a fearful position during the entire of that fateful night. I thought it more strange as the crew of the lifeboat were present, accompanied by Mr David McCutcheon of Tyrella, and from what I know of the kind and humane disposition of the latter gentleman, it is so unlike him to allow the men to leave the poor sufferer so long to his fate. I therefore called at the County Down Infirmary where the men were under treatment and inquired of themselves. Thompson, the man of colour who was also caught between the timber and the ship, was so far recovered as to be able to sit up, but Murray, who had been trapped by the logs all that dreadful night, was confined to his bed and was evidently suffering the most acute pain. They are both brave, manly fellows and I am happy to state that neither of them attach the slightest blame to anyone. Murray, who was on deck all night, caught by the leg like a rat in a trap, stated that he, and the other man Thompson were down between the logs and the bulwarks, fixing some ropes when the vessel struck and the shock caused the logs of timber to shift and caught their legs against the bulwarks; that the remaining men exerted themselves in all their power to release them, that they succeeded on extricating Thompson, but, owing to the weight of the logs and the fearful state of the sea, it was impossible for them to relieve him. I asked could they not have returned with additional help and got him off ? He said that it was quite impossible, that every wave was breaking right over and sweeping the vessel with such fearful force that he thought every minute his neck would have been broken or that he would have been smothered by the water; but that it would have been impossible for any person to have remained on deck, unless they had been lashed to the vessel. I am sure your readers, like me, will be greatly relieved to hear this statement from the lips of the brave sufferer himself who was in such a perilous position during the eight hours of that fearful night, as he said himself, expecting that every minute would be his last. The poor fellow's system has received such a shock as to render him (independent of the injury to his leg) unable to work for a long time. Surely this is a deserving case for the sympathy of the affluent. I regret to say that, through thoughtlessness, the two men, when being conveyed in an open cart to the Infirmary the following morning, were not provided with any covering but that of their wet clothes, same as they had spent the night in… (xvi)

The rest of the letter was an argument, based on this tragedy, for the need of a Harbour of Refuge at Ardglass – a topic of considerable controversy at the time. Ardglass and Carlingford were competing for government money to transform their fishing harbours into harbours big enough to accommodate up to medium sized ships.

The letter seems such a contradiction in many ways; it begins by accusing the crew and lifeboatmen of inhumanity because they left a trapped sailor to suffer all night, not knowing if he would be freed, but the letter then demonstrates, using the sufferer's own words, why help could not possibly have been given before it did. The final comment regarding the two injured sailors, put into an open cart in their wet clothes with all their injuries and subjected to the jolting they would have endured along the six miles of bumpy country dirt tracks from Ballyvaston to Downpatrick Infirmary, completed the picture of inhumanity. The letter was written by William Davidson, the Coroner of Downpatrick, and a man of considerable importance and social standing.

Not surprisingly, in the columns of the *Downpatrick Recorder* the following Saturday, there was a response to this letter… from not one but two correspondents. The first response came from David McCutcheon, a well-known and respected personage in the neighbourhood who had taken on the lease of Tyrella House and Demesne after AH Montgomery's death in 1867. He had continued the tradition established by Montgomery of loaning the horses required to pull the lifeboat carriage, and, on occasions such as this, of horsing them himself. He was clearly very annoyed by the accusations made by the Coroner:

Dear Sir, I was astounded to read a letter in your issue of last Saturday, signed William Davidson, concerning the wreck of the *Donna Maria*, the object of which is evidently to cast blame on all present on that awful occasion. Now, for the sake of the men connected with the lifeboat, as well as others in the neighbourhood I, with your permission, will state the real facts of the case, and the public can then judge whether the strictures and condemnations of the Coroner are warranted by the circumstances.

When notice of the jeopardy of the *Donna Maria* reached Tyrella, the people were in bed; they had to be raised and the boat drawn by horses over two miles and when at the nearest point to the vessel, the boat was launched; from the raging of the sea and the fury of the storm, for a considerable time it was feared that the boat would not reach the vessel, but by courage, skill and perseverance they at length succeeded, and rescued five poor fellows from the wreck, most unwillingly leaving one behind, who was so jambed by the shifting of some heavy logs of timber that he could not be relieved until tools were procured to cut away the part of the vessel where he was caught, the ship's saws having been swept overboard. Immediately, I went to a carpenter's half a mile distant where I procured two saws, but on returning to the scene of the disaster, the tide was so far out that it was utterly impossible after the most untiring exertions to get the boat, nearly 4 tons weight over the rocks; so that we had to most unwillingly wait till the tide was so far left the vessel that they could reach her without the boat. Then, with as little delay as possible, the poor fellow was relieved by John Gordon, the vice-coxswain of the lifeboat and carried ashore by the crew of that boat.

And now for the alleged cruel treatment of the injured parties, vis: the coloured seaman who had fallen overboard and the man who was so long in the wreck. All I can say is that a very poor man, James Armstrong, roused his feeble old mother out of her warm bed and there the poor injured sailors were made as comfortable as possible in the old woman's bed with all the bed clothes in the house over them, supplying them also with some warm tea, and there they remained until ready for removal to the County Infirmary. I cannot imagine what else Mr Davidson, even though Coroner, could have done if he had been present, through such an inclement night as I and others were, instead of in his comfortable bed in Downpatrick. (xvii)

The second correspondent was the Hon Secretary of the Tyrella Branch of the Lifeboat Institution, who had been disparagingly referred to in the closing line of Mr Davidson's original letter. The Rev Thomas Fielding Martin, rector of Tyrella parish had been over 60 years old when he accepted the incumbency in 1859; he had been associated with the lifeboat at Tyrella even before its inauguration and had taken over as Hon Secretary after the death of AH Montgomery. It is clear that the 77 year old had not lost the power to make a point in a very telling manner:

Sir, My attention has been called to a letter in the Recorder of last Saturday, signed William Davidson… relative to the wreck of the *Donna Maria* at Ballyvaston. In reply to his remarks, permit me to say that it never entered the head of the Hon Sec that it

(28) A lifeboat crew and horses c1866.

could be supposed by any sane individual that the man could be left in suffering if there was any possibility of preventing it, or of relieving the sufferer; but it required the astute comprehension of Mr Davidson to discover a flaw in the humane proceedings and gallant rescue on the night of the 28th ult.

On that night, in the midst of a whole gale, accompanied by bitter and incessant rain, the Tyrella lifeboat was taken from her house at 1.15am, and with her crew and launchers, arrived at the scene of the wreck, a distance of nearly three miles at 2.15am, when she was launched; after a most severe pull, they reached the vessel, but had great difficulty in taking the men on board on account of the heavy seas at the time. As regards the suffering man, James Murray, I would observe that all the boat's crew, if they could have been spared the management of her, would not have been sufficient to free him from his perilous situation.

They left for the shore thereafter at 3.15 am with those already rescued to procure tools and help to liberate Murray. After landing, the poor perishing mariners were helped to Minerstown, nearly a mile distant where they were housed at Denis McMullan's. Carpenter's tools were then procured from Henry Murphy, and by 6.30am the men were again on board with plenty of help to assist in raising the heavy timber. After two hours severe labour with wedges, hatchets and saws, the sufferer was at last extricated and brought to the cabin of James Armstrong, where he was put in Armstrong's own bed and had warm tea given to him. The vice-coxswain would have given him brandy but Dr Harrison would not permit it.

And now sir, I would suggest that your correspondent should watch for an opportunity of being present at a wreck by night and taking part in the rescue. He would then learn something of what 'Lifeboat work' is, and the dangers and hardships attending to it. I would remark that he cannot do better than act at once on his own benevolent suggestion by collecting a fund and heading it with a liberal subscription for the benefit of the injured man now in Down Infirmary, whom he justly designated a 'deserving case'. It is to be lamented that there is not an agent for the Shipwrecked Mariners Society on this coast and that therefore those rescued from a watery grave are thrown upon the charity of the miserably poor cottiers along the shore. If our Lifeboat were liberally supported by the gentry, wealthy merchants and wealthy inhabitants, there might accrue a surplus to meet the necessities of those saved but, as it is, there is not much more than half the sum required for its support subscribed in aid of our Tyrella Lifeboat. (xviii)

Together, the letters showed the dogged determination of the lifeboatmen to get back to the injured man, even trying to haul the lifeboat over rocks, rather than wait for the tide to ebb out. The phrase 'miserable cottiers' is a stark reminder of the extreme poverty that existed in parts of rural Ireland, even as late as the 1870's. Despite his own circumstances, James Armstrong gave what he could in allowing the injured sailors to rest and get warm, until they could travel to the Infirmary. The lack of covering, or of a more salubrious vehicle to carry them to Down Infirmary was not due to thoughtlessness but poverty. The cart was all there was, and the bedcoverings that had covered the men were no doubt being dried in front of a fire to be used that night – they could not be spared to cover the sailors. That the Rev Martin was annoyed was understandable; he had been present at many wrecks and had seen the attendant dangers and hardships for both the lifeboatmen and the rescued. He would have understood that unless people had witnessed a rescue they could not know what was involved, but in the Rev Martin's eyes, such people should not then pass judgement on what happened at the rescue. The action of the Levite in passing by on the other side, was undoubtedly how he saw William Davidson… someone else will always do it. Hence not only the call on Davidson to attend a rescue but also the Rev Martin's remark that the Coroner should act on his own suggestion and set up a fund for the injured man, and, using his social position, encourage others to contribute to it. This would then be true Christian action, not just pious platitudes.

Not surprisingly the following week brought a letter from William Davidson who had clearly been nettled, expressing himself surprised that the two gentlemen had taken so much umbrage to his stating the facts; however, because no-one denied that the two sailors had been conveyed in a cart with no covering he was able to repeat his initial assertion that such treatment was quite unchristian and inhumane. No further letters followed, and no record can be found as to whether or not a fund was set up for the injured man, or his final fate.

The touchiness of Rev Martin about the Tyrella lifeboat was of long standing, his concerns having already been noted in the Inspector's report of December 1873. Having taken on the mantle of Hon Secretary after AH Montgomery's death (a post he held till his own retirement in 1877, due to ill-health) he found it much harder to secure the annual funding than AH Montgomery had. While Montgomery was Secretary, the Branch easily secured their annual running costs, as expected by the National Lifeboat Institution. The Rev Martin soon found that the social influence of Montgomery, as Treasurer of the County Down, and a Magistrate, could secure funding that a country parson could not. In the accounts for 1868, the major donors in the list of subscribers published were the local gentry, headed by the Marquis of Downshire, Lord de Ros, Lord Viscount Bangor and the Montgomery's of Greyabbey (Lady Amelia and Hugh Montgomery); there were few payments from ordinary citizens and in his first report as Branch Secretary, the Rev Martin reflected:

> I cannot hope to make our Branch self-supporting in the current year, unless our subscriptions are increased… but where so much money has been expended of late by our gentry, commercial friends &c in providing recreation for the masses by way of races, steeplechases &c, I trust it will be only necessary to name the above fact to secure from those parties upon whose benevolence, from their prosperity and position in this part of the country, our Tyrella Branch has a very strong claim, that countenance and support which an Institution so valuable in saving human life is so justly entitled. Much has been done in the name of pleasure – I pray that something may now be done in the way of duty. (xix)

By July 1872, the finances of the Tyrella Branch had not only not improved, they had got worse. In a letter accompanying the publication of the accounts the Rev Martin wrote:

> …the funds of the Branch are very low, so low that the aid of the humane, who can sympathise with the shipwrecked mariner in all his suffering and sorrows is earnestly requested. The chief desire of the National Lifeboat Institution is that our branch (in its ordinary expenses) should be self-supporting. This object cannot be effected, however, by a less sum than 30 guineas per annum and yet our subscription for the last year did not exceed £19. Surely the difference after all is but a small amount for our resident gentry,

merchants and others who possess property in the district extending from Dundrum to Clough, Seaforde, Downpatrick and Killough to make up. (xx)

The frustration of the Rev Martin is palpable, and almost certainly explains his thinly veiled sarcasm in response to William Davidson who, while publicly expressing his concern for the shipwrecked men and their fate, was never a subscriber to the Tyrella lifeboat.

When the Rev Martin retired as the rector of Tyrella, the regional and local press reported on the presentation made to him:

Of all the public works that Mr Martin engaged in, and they were many, there was none of greater importance than the exertions he made to get a lifeboat for Tyrella and to have it successfully operated. I am glad to find that not only locally but nationally have his exertions been recognised; for I find here a resolution passed by the National Lifeboat Institution, of which Her Majesty is patron, so late as 4 April 1878, thanking Mr Martin for his great exertions. When a National Institution so recognises his labours in the cause, I think Tyrella and the country may be proud of Mr Martin's work and of the means he used to save valuable lives which otherwise might have been lost, but

TYRELLA BRANCH.

Honorary Secretary—
Rev. T. F. MARTIN, M.A.

Annual Subscriptions.

	£	s	d
The Marquis of Down-shire	5	0	0
The Dowager Marchioness of Down-shire	1	0	0
Viscount Bangor	2	0	0
The Lady Amelia Montgomery	1	0	0
The Lady Matilda Montgomery	1	1	0
Lord de Ros	2	0	0
Atkinson, J. Brooke, Esq.	–	10	0
Birney, Capt., Oakly Park	–	10	0
Digney, Mr. Patrick	–	5	0
East Downshire S. S. Co. Dundrum, per Mr. E.G.Hennesay	2	2	0
Hudson, Mrs. R. R..	–	5	0
Montgomery, Hugh, Esq.	2	10	0
Murland, Sam. Esq..	–	10	0
Nugent, Maj.Andrew	1	0	0
Poë, William T. Esq.	1	0	0
Reid, J. Esq.	–	10	0
Russell, C. Esq. J.P.	–	10	0
Waulfe, S. R. Esq. ..	1	1	0
Total	£22	14	0

(29) & (30) Subscriptions for Tyrella Branch

TYRELLA BRANCH.

Honorary Secretary—A. H. MONTGOMERY, Esq.

	£ s d	£ s d		£ s d	£ s d
The Duchess of —— .	10 0 0		Brought forward .	63 0 0	15 0 0
The Marquis of Downshire .	10 0 0	5 0 0	Freke, the Rev. J. H. . .	1 0 0	
The Marchioness of Down-shire		1 0 0	Gordon, Robert, Esq. .	1 0 0	
The Earl of Macclesfield . .	5 0 0		Gordon, the Rev. James . .	3 0 0	
The Dowager Countess of Macclesfield	1 0 0		Hall, Roger, Esq. . . .	2 0 0	
The Earl of Hillsborough .		1 0 0	Hamilton, Capt. . . .	1 0 0	
Viscount Bangor . . .	5 0 0	2 0 0	Hall, the Rev. Francis H. . .	2 0 0	
The Lady Amelia Montgomery	2 0 0	1 0 0	Hamill, Miss Catherine . .	5 0 0	
The Lady Charlotte Montgomery . .	2 0 0		Keown, William, Esq. .		1 0 0
The Lady Louisa Parker .	0 10 0		Maxwell, J. W., Esq. . .	5 0 0	1 0 0
Lord de Ros . .		2 0 0	Montgomery, A. H., Esq. .	5 0 0	2 0 0
Forde, Colonel, M.P. .	5 0 0	2 0 0	Montgomery, Hugh, Esq. .	2 10 0	2 10 0
Ker, D. S., Esq., M.P. .	5 0 0		Nugent, Major	1 0 0	
Montgomery, Lieut.-Colonel.	2 0 0		Price, James B., Esq. .		0 10 0
Birney, John, Esq. .	10 0 0	1 0 0	Pilson, Conway, Esq. . .	2 0 0	
Bailie, James, Esq. .	1 0 0		Reilly, J. T., Esq. . .	1 0 0	
Crozier, Thomas, Esq. .	1 0 0		Ridge, Capt., R.N. .		1 0 0
Cleland, James, Esq. .	1 0 0		Smyth, Henry, Esq. . .	3 3 0	
De Salis, John, Esq. .	2 10 0		Ward, T. L., Esq. . .	1 0 0	
			Sundry Small Sums . .	3 8 6	
			Total. . .	102 1 6	23 0 0

(31) Memorial
in Tyrella parish
church to Rev.
TF Martin.

In Loving Memory of
REV. THOMAS FIELDING MARTIN, M.A.,
FOR 20 YEARS
RECTOR OF TYRELLA.
BORN 28TH JUNE 1797.
DIED 14TH SEPT 1879.

Resurgam.

ERECTED BY THE PARISHIONERS
AS A TOKEN OF GRATITUDE.

for the establishment of this lifeboat which has hitherto been so effectively worked by the present coxswain, vice-coxswain and crew....A presentation was made by the coxswain Mr John Gordon, and the vice-coxswain Mr Joseph Mitchell, of a beautiful ebony walking stick, mounted in silver and bearing an appropriate inscription. (xxi)

Sadly the Rev. Martin died the following year in 1879, aged 82. The parishioners of Tyrella subscribed to a memorial plaque in the church to honour him.

However, the succession of letters and the war of words over the fate of the injured seamen on the *Donna Maria* did not affect the decision of the RNLI to award:

…the silver medal of the society and its thanks on vellum… to Adam Murphy coxswain of the Tyrella lifeboat and to John Gordon, the assistant coxswain, for their gallant service in the boat and particularly on the occasion of the lifeboat saving the crew of the *Donna Maria* of Belfast, which was wrecked in Dundrum Bay during a heavy gale from the south east on 29 November 1874. (xxii)

The RNLI also awarded its Thanks on Vellum (the equivalent of a Bronze Medal) to Robert Foland, the coastguard who pulled the coloured seaman out of the sea when he fell in crossing to the lifeboat. There was a very real danger for anyone who fell between a lifeboat and the ship they were leaving; the force of the waves could dash them against one or other boat or they could be crushed before being rescued. Robert Foland could have overbalanced or been dragged in trying to effect the rescue, hence the award by the RNLI.

Fame is fleeting; the day after the *Donna Maria* was wrecked, the lifeboat was called out again to rescue the crew of an un-named vessel that had capsized in Dundrum Bay, in the heavy gale that had blown for a number of days. Few details were given in the newspaper report other than the vessel was bound for Whitehaven, but what port it had left, what its cargo was or how many crew it carried are unknown.

That was not unusual for the time; reports on disasters at sea depended on someone, sometimes a Lloyd's agent, sometimes a Coastguard or member of the public, informing the newspaper. Shipping losses were notoriously understated for that reason.

Some rescues, however, were well documented, such as the next 'shout' for *The Tyrella* which featured in *The Lifeboat*:

During the afternoon of 26 February 1875, the lifeboat *Tyrella*, in answer to signals of distress was launched to the assistance of the schooner *Friends*, of Killyleagh, which vessel having had all her sails blown away while on a voyage from Girvan to Killyleagh, came to anchor in Dundrum Bay in an easterly gale. The sea in the Bay was much broken and

(32) Close-up shot of Silver Medal for gallantry.

the master of the schooner, expecting the vessel to flounder at her anchor, hoisted signals calling for succour. The coxswain being absent, the lifeboat went out in charge of John Gordon, the second coxswain, who succeeded in bringing the whole of the vessel's crew – four in number – safely on shore. The Tyrella strand is much exposed in an easterly gale and the task of getting the Lifeboat off it, in face of an on-shore gale is always one of difficulty, especially on account of the sparsity of population in that neighbourhood, rendering it a work of time to collect a number of launchers. (xxiii)

The final rescue for the second Tyrella lifeboat in October 1875, involved a Laxey steamer, the *Lizzie*, carrying coal from Swansea to Belfast, which got into difficulties in Dundrum Bay; the master called for help. The lifeboat went out and rescued the crew, although there was no indication of how many were saved. The master took the decision to beach the vessel in the hope of saving the cargo; a Board of Trade enquiry was held to investigate the circumstances surrounding the stranding of the vessel, and the master was exonerated of negligent navigation. The cargo was safely discharged, but the ship was so badly damaged that she was auctioned at the site of her stranding, Ballyvaston.

It was commonplace to auction off a badly damaged ship and all its contents at the site of the wreck in order to realise as much capital for the owners/investors; the columns of local newspapers carried notice of such auctions a week in advance, giving directions if the site was in a more remote location.

SALES BY AUCTION.

SHIPWRECKED STEAMER FOR SALE.

To be Sold by Public AUCTION (on account of whom it may concern), on TUESDAY next, the 2nd prox., at TEN o'clock precisely, on the Beach where she now lies stranded in DUNDRUM BAY, about a mile inside St. John's Point,

THE HULL of the S.S. LIZZIE, of Douglas, Isle of Man, 264 Tons net register, about 400 Tons burthen; built and engined by LAIRD, of Birkenhead. Also, at the same time and place, the CARGO on board and the MATERIAL and GEAR landed from said Vessel. This Steamer had new Boilers in 1872, and over £4,000 was spent on her in extensive repair and improvements in the present year.

She will be Sold as she may lie on the beach at date of Sale ; terms and conditions then.

Passengers by the 7.30 train from Belfast to Downpatrick (where cars will attend on arrival) can reach the Wreck in good time for Sale.

SINCLAIR & BOYD, Agents for Lloyd's, &c.

HUGH HAMILTON, Auctioneer.

Donegall Quay, Belfast,
26th October, 1875.

(33) Shipwreck auction notice.

80

Chapter 6:
The *Memorial*

In June 1875 the Rev TF Martin, as Hon Secretary, reported to the National Lifeboat Institution that there were concerns about the condition of the lifeboat. The Assistant Inspector visited the station in July and found three planks on one side and two on the other to be deficient. As she was nearly 10 years old, the Assistant Inspector recommended that she be replaced. The committee agreed, ordered the boat from Messrs Woolfe & Son and decided:

> …to appropriate the new lifeboat to the Misses Peach of Derby, who by means of fancy needlework &c had presented £400 to the Institution to defray the cost of a lifeboat to be named the *Memorial*. (i)

The boat had its harbour trials in November and was dispatched on December 10 to Tyrella. Its journey was at first uneventful, following the usual routine of being conveyed free of charge to Fleetwood by the London and North-Western Railway, then free of charge to Belfast on one of the steamers of the North Lancashire Steam Navigation Company. However, a problem of the further transportation of the lifeboat from Belfast to Tyrella became apparent:

> December 14: the lifeboat arrived this morning and was disembarked and conveyed to the Country Down Railway station. The Assistant Inspector found that some of the Arches across the line were too low for the safety of the Boat as the trucks were higher than those generally used on other lines. He therefore arranged for her conveyance by road. This was somewhat difficult at this time of year, as all the large carrier firms were very much pressed with work and had all their horses employed. It was however, at last accomplished by two firms working together. The distance being 34 miles (English), the lowest price at which the Assistant Inspector could procure the services of six horses was £24. The lifeboat proceeded this day as far as Downpatrick (23 miles) where the night was spent and on the following morning the remainder of the journey was accomplished, and the boat safely reached Tyrella.

The old boat and transporting carriage were returned to London. The minutes record that the "lifeboat was launched with the usual ceremonies and although the weather was threatening, it held up at the time and everyone seemed pleased with the boat."(ii)

On 1st January 1876 the following notice appeared in the *Downpatrick Recorder*:

On 17th December ult, the National Lifeboat Institution, through their Assistant Inspector, Captain Robertson, presented the Tyrella station with a new lifeboat, the old boat having been worn out in service. Those invited gathered in the Boat House, whilst a speech was made about the previous boats and their crews since 1860 – not one shipwrecked person had been lost in the Bay since that time. The boat has been presented to the Institution by the Misses Peach, of Langley Hall, Derbyshire. On their request the boat was named the *Memorial*. The Rector's wife, Mrs Martin, performed the naming ceremony. (iii)

Of the four Royal National Lifeboat Institution boats at Tyrella, the *Memorial* had the most launches and saved the most lives in its twelve years on station.

Its first 'shout' was literally the day after the ceremonies were reported in the papers; the *Ellen* was driven ashore, near the Black Rock at Rathmullen, in a strong SE gale and the lifeboat was horsed to a spot near to the ship and launched. However, ultimately its services were not required, and it returned to the boat house. The next 'shout' for the new boat came in November 1876:

A French brig, the *Aulini Sinai*, laden with grain, was driven on the Dolly Rocks in Dundrum Bay this morning. The *Memorial* lifeboat of the National Lifeboat Station proceeded to the spot and was instrumental in saving the crew of six men from the wreck. The boat behaved well on this her first real service… This boat is of much larger dimensions than the one formerly in use at this station. On this occasion it was horsed by Mr David McCutcheon of Tyrella who has frequently rendered important services when wrecks occurred in Dundrum Bay. Since the lifeboat was established here in 1860 it has been instrumental in saving 52 lives. (iv)

David McCutcheon's 10 year tenancy of Tyrella House and Demesne ended in 1877 and the estate was sold. RNLI minutes noted on September 6, 1877:

Committee voted the Thanks of the Institution inscribed on vellum to Mr D McCutcheon who had provided horses for the lifeboat on all occasions of service during the last 10 years, sometimes without making any charges for the same and who was about to leave the neighbourhood. (v)

(34) Service book for the *Memorial*.

Change also soon followed when Adam Murphy retired as Coxswain in 1877, the RNLI presenting him with £5 and an inscribed telescope in recognition of his time spent as Coxswain of the Tyrella lifeboat. John Gordon took over as coxswain and Joseph Mitchell became assistant coxswain, Gordon remaining as coxswain of the Tyrella lifeboats until the station closed.

In April 1877 the lifeboat responded in a south-easterly gale with very rough seas, to signals of distress from *Ocean Packet No 3* of Harlingen. When the lifeboat got to the brigantine, they found it abandoned; some accounts have the ship seeking safety in Newcastle, where the crew disembarked….it is probable that the boat broke its moorings in the gale that continued to rage. Some 12 months after this, in April 1878, the lifeboat was called out to the schooner *Cygnet*, driven ashore in very heavy seas, close to the Coastguard Station. Her crew of four were safely rescued. Later that year, in September, the lifeboat rescued the crew of three from the *Wasp*, which stranded at Tyrella as it was carrying coal from Troon to Newry. In November 1880, the lifeboat went out to the brig *Olaf Kyrie* in a severe south- easterly gale, but the wind shifted south-westerly, enabling her to weather St John's Point, and the lifeboat returned to station.

A gap of 18 months elapsed before her services were required again. The next 'shout' for the *Memorial* was in February 1881, this time to the brig *Bransty* of Whitehaven, heading to Penarth with oats. She was wrecked on the Long Rocks, almost within view of the Boat House, during a severe gale and a very heavy sea. The *Memorial* had great difficulty in getting off the beach because of the force of the breakers, but, under the command of the new coxswain, John Gordon, rescued the crew of four; the master broke his leg getting into the lifeboat. In September of that year, the barque *Gertrude* was stranded on rocks close to Minerstown. The Tyrella lifeboat came alongside and took off those members of the crew that wanted to leave – some thirteen did so; the master, chief officer and three other crew refused to leave. It took a full week before the barque could be re-floated. A subsequent Board of Trade Inquiry found the master guilty of negligent navigation and suspended his licence; the length of suspension was not mentioned. In December of 1881 the lifeboat spent hours searching in heavy fog and a deep swell for a ship whose distress signals had been clearly seen but nothing was found.

There was an obvious camaraderie, and gentle rivalry between the Newcastle and Tyrella lifeboat stations; the presence of the *Memorial* with her crew at the launch in October 1881 of the new lifeboat in Newcastle, the *Farnley* (replacing the *Reigate* which had been in service since 1859) was noted with much approval in a Belfast newspaper. However, the newspaper's concluding comment gives an insightful reflection on the need for lifeboats in the area – Tyrella station was less than six miles across the Bay from Newcastle:

> …neither State subsidy nor Government grant but voluntary contributions support an organisation so extensive; a subscription may have been dropped by the summer visitor into the boxes which here and there receive the mites given for the great fleet of lifeboats and the furtherance of the society's noble work. The necessity for such an Institution cannot be seen in the middle of summer, but when the fashionable watering place [Newcastle] becomes the fishing village and Slieve Donard is wrapped in mists; when the waves break in thunder on the rocks and cover the beach with foam, the lifeboatmen hold themselves in readiness. (vi)

Ships were not just casualties of the severe winter gales at Tyrella, but also of late summer storms. (See Appendix 6 for a Table showing seasonal occurrence of wrecks at Tyrella). An article entitled "Narrow Escape of a British North American Ship" which appeared in a Belfast paper in August 1883, outlined a long and arduous call out for the *Memorial*:

The ship *Henry*, commanded by Captain J White, with a crew of twenty-four, left Liverpool with a general cargo, bound for New Brunswick and had a narrow escape in Dundrum Bay. The captain's intention was to take the North Channel, and, in this attempt, he was caught by a strong south-east gale, which increased on Monday morning, accompanied by rain. About 6 o'clock on Monday evening, breakers were seen ahead, whence the ship's course was at once brought up short to the wind, on the starboard tack. Breakers were, however, reported on the bow, and the men being at their stations, the helm was put down so as to give the vessel an opposite tack; owing to the heavy sea that was running, she would not come around, and there was no room to move.

In this dilemma the only thing that could be done was to let go both anchors and when about 100 fathoms of cable had been expended, the anchors hit the ground. The sails were devied up and furled, and the weather having slightly abated, it was only then that the men on board realised the dangerous nature of their position. It was found that there was high land distant about one mile off while the sea was breaking on the rocks close beside the ship, which had drifted under St John's Point in the Bay of Dundrum. Captain Pugh RN, Inspecting Commander of Coastguards in the District was speedily on the spot and dispatched one of his men to Tyrella, four miles distant, for the lifeboat crew. Shortly after, Mr John Gordon (coxswain) launched the craft amidst weather which was extremely severe.

The lifeboat having got alongside, everything was done to ease the ship during Tuesday night. At daylight on the next (Wednesday) morning the wind veered round to the West with a heavy sea. The crew seemed determined to get the ship underway, rather than risk another dreadful night and in this they were assisted by two tugs, *Shamrock* and *Protector*, that had been dispatched from Belfast the previous day, but were compelled to seek shelter in Donaghadee in consequence of the severity of the weather. The anchors were eventually weighed, the tugs cast off and the lifeboat with its fatigued crew returned to the shore about 10 o'clock yesterday… with five fishermen who had boarded the ship *Henry* and had no means of getting ashore, their boat having been cut away by the heavy seas. (vii)

Even though the crew had been on active duty for well over 24 hours, the lifeboat had to be put back on its carriage, horsed back to the Boat House and safely stowed away, ready for immediate use. (Rules 21 and 22 of the Lifeboat Regulations)

Sadly, not all rescues ended successfully, although up to 1884, as far as records show, the

(35) A similar scene to the Victoria, close to shore crowds and lifeboat; rocket was not launched in 1884.

Tyrella Lifeboats had not lost a crew member, or failed to save anyone they set out to rescue. However, that record was most tragically broken on 16 February 1884 when the *Victoria*, of Beaumaris, carrying slates, ran aground on the rocks at Rathmullen, in a heavy gale. The night must have been very dark, as the wreck site was close to the Coastguard Station, but nothing was seen until daylight, when three of the crew were seen in the rigging. The Tyrella lifeboat was immediately sent for and launched. Mr Bowles, chief officer of the Tyrella Coastguard and two men arrived with lifebelts and lifelines; one of the coastguards, Alexander Moody, crept out as far on the rocks as he could go and tried throwing the lifeline several times. The wind kept whipping it back and it failed to reach the ship or the men on board. Eventually, the spars to which the sailors were clinging, gave way and the unfortunate men were plunged into the raging surf, perishing within 100 yards of land and within both sight and hearing of the spectators on shore. They were unable to help them, there being no apparatus or rocket launchers that could be used. The Tyrella lifeboat, under its coxswain John Gordon, arrived just after the men had fallen off the rigging, but despite their best efforts they could not rescue them.

Not surprisingly, given the large number of people who had watched helplessly as the tragedy

(36) Rocket Launcher.

unfolded, two questions were the subject of a letter, published in local newspapers. The writer, under the pseudonym of CONCERNED, praised the coastguards for their bravery in trying to reach the men on the rigging but questioned why they had not been equipped with rocket launchers, rather than lifelines that the wind kept throwing back. CONCERNED was also fulsome in his praise for the efforts of the lifeboat when it reached the scene and the thorough manner in which the lifeboatmen searched for the sailors that had fallen from the rigging but questioned why the lifeboat could not be propelled by steam power. This, the writer believed, would have meant that the lifeboat would not have had to be horsed on its carriage close to the site of the wreck and then launched from the beach; it could have proceeded, under steam power, from the Boat House and so arrived at the scene much faster, possibly in time to have saved the men.

A decade earlier, Richard Lewis had provided the answer to just such a question:

> A lifeboat, like the stormy petrel which is rarely seen when the heavens are calm and the sea smooth, has its work to do amidst broken seas and curling surf, where no other boat can live. Lifeboats go through heavy seas, often filling the boat to the level of the thwarts from 3 – 4 tons of water frequently breaking into a lifeboat from a single wave. It will thus be readily conceived by those who have never seen a lifeboat that there would be extreme difficulties in sufficiently protecting the fires of steam boats from being extinguished.

(37) A Dangerous Rescue

Also, the extremely violent motion to which boats are often subjected – sometimes thrown into a vertical position or lateral movement even more violent, there couldn't be fire for a steam propeller to work; moreover, there is too shallow a draught on a lifeboat which would not allow a decent screw-propeller to be fitted. Finally, the only men available as volunteers to man lifeboats are fishermen; they do not have the necessary experience to manage a steam engine and keep it in perfect order. (viii)

Not with-standing the technical improvements being made in an era of rapid innovation, steam lifeboats were not to be a feature of the RNLI fleet. The first one, launched in 1890 and called the *Duke of Northumberland*, saw service but was one of only a few ever built, as, in the early years of the 20th century, the introduction of the motor engine completely revolutionised the Lifeboat service.

Almost exactly a year after the tragedy of the *Victoria*, the brigantine *Mary Helen* got into difficulties in a south easterly gale but declined the assistance of the lifeboat which had been alerted to the ship's plight by the Tyrella Coastguard. In February 1885, a schooner, the *Helen of Leith*, carrying coals to Rostrevor, was driven, in a dreadful gale, onto the sands at Tyrella, close to the Coastguard Station. The *Memorial* was called out and succeeded in rescuing the crew of four. Just a few months later, in August 1885, in another dreadful south-easterly gale, the schooner, *Rambler*, was driven onto the rocks that jut out into the sea from the Coastguard Station at Ringsallin Point. The schooner was:

> …in imminent peril for a couple of hours. The Tyrella lifeboat, *Memorial*, responded to its signals of distress and the lifeboat was sighted, making its way through the sea, the waves at times almost completely immersing it. On coming up to the wreck, the greatest danger was experienced in taking off the crew and as the captain was crossing the rail he was blown into the sea, but fortunately he was rescued, having sustained little injury. After a passage of extreme peril, the *Memorial* landed her living freight at Dundrum and the shipwrecked carried in an exhausted state to the Sailor's Home. (ix)

Another newspaper, which had also reported the story added:

> Great difficulty was experienced in getting alongside the vessel on account of the rocks and great danger was incurred by the lifeboatmen who behaved splendidly. But for their timely service, the shipwrecked crew would no doubt have been lost, as the sea was breaking over the ship and no other boat, other than a lifeboat could possibly have succeeded on rescuing her. (x)

The *Downpatrick Recorder* noted that this was the 23rd rescue for John Gordon in the *Memorial*.

The following year, in the middle of an atrocious storm in March 1886, the schooner *Barclay* got itself into serious trouble in Dundrum Bay; the seamanship and bravery of the lifeboat crew who went out to its rescue was so remarkable as to warrant not just local and regional, but national press coverage, some of it very dramatic:

> On Sunday night, during a severe gale with heavy seas, lights were seen on Smith's Rock, a short distance to the south side of Tyrella, Co Down. (xi)

Smith's Rock lies a short distance from another rocky outcrop called Stinker Rock and these lie a very short distance from the Lifeboat House; under reasonable sea conditions it would have taken 15 minutes for the lifeboat to row out to it.

(38) Snowstorm at Tyrella. Smith's Rock and Stinker Rock in the background.

The night was pitchy dark and a snowstorm, driven by a south-east gale was raging. As soon as the distressed vessel was observed, the crew of the Tyrella lifeboat were quickly mustered and after several ineffectual attempts to put off to sea, they at last succeeded and the gallant boat and crew sped on their errand of mercy. The sea, which was running mountains high, and the furious head wind, proved more than a match for the lifeboat men, and despite their almost superhuman exertions, they were beaten back and finally driven ashore. They were not, however, totally conquered, and as there were plenty of brave men on the beach who gladly volunteered their assistance, and with additional hands on board, and double-banked oars, the gallant fellows once more put off to the rescue. This time they combated the elements successfully, and after a long hard pull, succeeded in reaching the stranded vessel. At this point, the utmost caution and coolness were required as the vessel was lying between two ranges of rocks, which were so close on either side as to render the boat's position extremely perilous. The darkness which was intense rendered the boat's position all the more dangerous as it was almost impossible to see the rocks. After the vessel's crew of five men and the captain's two children, a little boy and girl, were taken on board the lifeboat, the return journey to shore was commenced.

This also was attended with considerable danger as the boat had to pull right off to sea and come to shore by a circuitous route in order to avoid several ranges of rocks that lay between the vessel and the beach. At 10.30 o'clock, after three hours battling with the waves, the boat was safely beached, without accident of any kind. Had it not been for the manner in which the vessel's crew kept up lights, the lifeboat could not have found her position. The sailors' clothes, saturated with petroleum oil, were kept blazing and by this means their position was seen. Great credit is due to Mr Joseph Mitchell, the Lifeboat's second coxswain, who had charge of the boat, who, whilst showing the greatest courage, also displayed very marked ability in his skilful handling of the boat. The crew to a man bore out their now famous character for true pluck and endurance. Mr Bowles, chief officer of the Coastguards at Tyrella also rendered assistance of the most valuable kind by helping to get the boat out, and heartily encouraging the brave fellows to do their duty. The rescue throughout was of the most dangerous character to the lifeboatmen and was so skilfully and successfully conducted as to reflect the highest credit on all concerned. This now famous boat, the *Memorial*, behaved splendidly and thoroughly maintained her character for being truly a life-boat. (xii)

Lifeboat Regulations stipulated that crews should be drawn from the local fishermen and mariners who volunteered. The assistant coxswain, Joseph Mitchell was a Coastguard stationed at Tyrella and knew the area well. The seamanship displayed in this rescue is a good example as to why local knowledge was essential to any chance of a successful outcome to a rescue; the area of coast around Smith's Rock has several rocky reefs, hidden by a high tide, that would have ripped the hull of the lifeboat, had it hit them. The need for extra weight in the boat to help it cut through the waves, rather than be bounced around by them, is also why ballast was so important to a lifeboat and why it was possible to double-bank the oars and still take on persons rescued.

Just over a week later a report, based on an interview with three of the crew of the *Barclay* was published in their home city of Hull:

They were driven ashore on the rocks and the sea swept the decks from stem to stern; the men could not launch any of their boats, as they could not have survived in that sea; they had to signal as best they could in the darkness, in the hope of attracting the attention of people on shore; this the shipwrecked men did by making torches of their clothes. For about three hours these means were resorted to, until they had scarcely any clothing left. The Lifeboat authorities on shore had seen the signals and put off through the heavy surf. The gallant fellows were beaten back once; but nothing daunted they made the second attempt and were successful in rescuing all on board, seven in number, including the two children of the captain. The shipwrecked people were carefully attended to on the Irish coast. (xiii)

In March 1886 RNLI Records show:

Assistant Inspector visited station to enquire into the circumstances attending the launch of the lifeboat to the rescue of the schooner *Barclay* of Goole on the night of 27th February. He considered the service was a good one, well performed, the chief element of danger being the difficulty of ascertaining on such an extremely dark night the exact position of the many rocks. He considered Joseph Mitchell the 2nd coxswain who took command of the boat on this occasion had performed his duty well. The Coastguard authorities called the attention of the Institution to Mitchell's services on this occasion. (xiv)

However, no award was made to Joseph Mitchell. The RNLI Annual Report 1875 commented on how awards were decided:

The Committee devote much careful consideration to the granting of these awards. Each case is minutely inquired into, in the first instance through the co-operation of the officers of coastguard, the local Hon Sec and other responsible persons; and afterwards they are thoroughly scrutinised by the preparatory Committee, previous to their being sanctioned by the General Committee. (xv)

The rescue was considered meritorious enough to be investigated, but obviously at the time other rescues were judged to be more deserving of Awards.

The final 'shout' for the *Memorial* was on 26 January 1887, when the French barque, *Esperance*, with a cargo of teak, went down in Dundrum Bay. Reports cite a heavy sea and fog, through which the lifeboat successfully battled to take off the crew of ten men. The reports indicated that the vessel was likely to become a wreck, but its ultimate fate was not reported. No other call-outs for the lifeboat were reported, and it was replaced in 1888.

Chapter 7:
Swansong

The fourth, and last Royal National Lifeboat Institution lifeboat stationed at Tyrella, arrived on 7 June 1888, as the *Belfast News Letter* reported:

> The National Lifeboat Institution has just sent a new lifeboat to Tyrella to take the place of the one stationed there many years since. The new boat is 34 feet long, 7 ½ feet wide and rows 12 oars double-banked; it was built by Messrs Watkins & Co of Blackwall, London and possesses all the latest improvements, including water ballast fittings, which consist of two tanks amidships, one or both of which can be filled with water or emptied at will in the space of one minute. The object is to increase the ballast and immersion of the boat and consequently her draught of water when launched, or in very shallow

(39) Although not Tyrella Station this picture of Courtown Ireland, bears a striking resemblance to it.

water. The lifeboat has all the other characteristics of the boats of the National Lifeboat Institution in the way of self-righting, self-ejecting water &c. The cost of the new lifeboat and equipment have been defrayed by a handsome gift received by the Institution from Mrs Cameron of Ripon – the wife of Captain Cameron RN, who was formerly Inspecting Commander of HM Coastguard at Newcastle, Co Down, the amount having been realised by the sale of her own work, assisted by friends. In accordance with her wishes, the boat is to be named the Louisa Burnaby; it is to be publicly named and launched at Dundrum on Wednesday next, under the superintendence of the District Inspector of Lifeboats, Lieutenant Tipping. (i)

A fun element to the launch day in June occurred when, after the ceremonies were over:

> The old and new Tyrella boats had a race under oars with the Newcastle lifeboat, the old Tyrella boat coming in first, which the District Inspector attributed to her being manned by a much better crew. (ii)

According to local press, the crew of the Newcastle lifeboat, the *Farnley*, which had turned up to welcome the new Tyrella lifeboat and the crews of the Tyrella boats were treated to a celebratory meal in a Dundrum hotel afterwards.

Even with the improvements Peake had made, lifeboats were heavy of necessity to allow them to get through big breakers, and with their curved iron keel, a lifeboat weighed anything between 3–4 tons; with this kind of weight, unless a boat had a slipway, the lifeboat and its carriage had to be 'horsed'.

> Horses played an important role in the work of the Institution, dragging lifeboats across cliff tops or beaches to their launching sites. For the launch itself, they were usually divided into two teams, one on either side of the carriage on which the lifeboat was transported; they were then driven into the sea, until they had manoeuvred the carriage in deep enough water for the lifeboat to float. In heavy seas this was dangerous work; quite a few horses were injured, and some were drowned. (iii)

> …but, in the days when they [lifeboats] had to be hauled by horses and human helpers, losses were not unknown among both, before the boats were successfully got to sea. The process nearly always entailed risk and there was the certainty of cold and drenching. (iv)

(40) Horses bringing in the lifeboat.

Obviously getting horses was very important to the lifeboat and coxswains often had local arrangements in place:

> From the middle of the 19th century onwards, horse-owners were required by law to make their animals available if they were needed to help with launching a lifeboat… most farmers were happy for their horses to be used, partly out of humanity, and partly because they were paid for the loan of their animals and given generous compensation if they were killed or injured… (v)

Getting sufficient horses for the lifeboat carriage had never been a problem for the Tyrella Station, as the horses had come from the stables of Tyrella House, as we have seen in previous chapters; from 1867-1877, Mr David McCutcheon (who had leased Tyrella House) took charge of the horses himself at many rescues. After his departure, the Branch had to make a new arrangement with a neighbouring farmer but were able to rely on a guaranteed supply of horses whenever the lifeboat was needed.

However, not everywhere was so fortunate; the difficulty in obtaining horses to assist in a launch in 1895 had been noted, after a complaint had been made in:

>…reference to the lifeboat at Cloughey, Co Down. The boat is stationed about two miles from the wreck; and as soon as the vessel was seen to be in danger, a signal was given for the Lifeboat to be launched. This was impossible owing to the state of the sea. It was then decided to have it taken by road on its carriage. A difficulty was experienced here too, as the people refused to supply horses. Consequently, from the time the signal was given to the time the boat was underway, an interval of 2½ hours had passed. (vi)

Lewis described a typical launch:

>The lifeboat is drawn to the water's edge, where the carriage is turned around to rear end, facing seaward. The crew then take their place in the boat, each rower in his place, with his oar over the side, ready to pull, with the coxswain at the helm. The carriage is then backed by men, or horses, or both, sufficiently far into the water to ensure the boat being afloat when she is run off her carriage, or if the ground be very soft, the carriage is first backed into the water before the crew get into the boat. When all is ready, the coxswain, watching for a favourable moment, gives the word and the boat, the keel of which rests on iron rollers, is run off rapidly into the water, with her bow facing the surf. (vii)

Launching a boat off an open beach was a difficult task, made even more difficult when the wheels of the carriage sank into soft sand. The first occasion that the new Tyrella lifeboat, the *Louisa Burnaby*, appeared in the press not just locally but nationally was three days after its launch – because of its participation in what the *Belfast Weekly News* called 'An Interesting Experiment':

>On Saturday last a trial was made at the Tyrella Lifeboat Station of an invention to prevent the wheels of the lifeboat transporting carriage from sinking in loose or soft sand. Anyone who has seen a lifeboat launched off a sandy shore, knows the labour the crew have, even with a strong team of horses, to drag the boat and carriage, which weighs at least 3 tons across the sand to the water's edge, the wheels sinking deeply in the soft sand. Lieutenant Tipping RN, the District Inspector of Lifeboats in Ireland has invented a way of reducing this labour. This is effected by attaching to each of the 6 foot wheels of the carriage, a chain of plates, which revolve with the wheels, laying an iron road 15 inches broad for

them to run over. The plates are each 3 feet 2 inches long, made up of ¼ inch steel and strongly hinged together. On each plate an iron angle is riveted to guide the wheel and prevent it from running off. To place them on the wheel, the chain of seven plates is laid flat on the ground in front of the wheels which are then drawn over them. The end of the hindmost plate is attached to the wheel, which, as it revolves carries the plates round over the top and down the front until the two ends of the chain of plates meet. They are then shackled together; this can be done in about five minutes. When the plates were adjusted, the boat and carriage were drawn over the sands, four horses taking them along at a good trot. The carriage was turned sharply without any difficulty, the plates only sinking 1/8th of an inch. The coxswain and crew were greatly pleased with the result and considered that with the plates twelve men could do as much as thirty men without them. Several militia officers and others were present and expressed themselves much pleased with

(41) Lifeboat carriage wheel with 'Tipping Plates'.

the results of the trial. There is little doubt that the adoption of these plates will greatly increase the usefulness of lifeboats. (viii)

Lieutenant Tipping almost certainly picked the new lifeboat and carriage at Tyrella to be used to showcase his invention, both because he had supervised its installation just before the experiment took place, and also because of the very soft sand over which the Tyrella lifeboat had to normally travel when being launched from any of the beaches in the area. His invention, which was an improvement on an 1856 invention by James Boydell, called the self-laying or endless railway, became known as the Tipping Plates and was widely used when launching off soft sand.

However, it is intriguing to note the interest shown in it by the militia officers, as the caterpillar tracks of the armoured Tank, which made its first appearance in the First World War, bear a resemblance to the interlocking Tipping Plates. (Lieutenant Tipping was by then Lieutenant–Commander Garside-Tipping RN, and was sadly killed in action on 25 September 1915, the oldest naval officer serving afloat.)

The first 'shout' for the *Louisa Burnaby* was:

> …the *Wild Rose*, a comparatively new iron screw steamer engaged in the coasting trade… going to Cardiff from Donaghadee. When off Dundrum, she was seen flying distress signals. The Tyrella lifeboat put off and rescued part of the crew and landed them at Dundrum.

News of this shipwreck had reached the paper by telegram and the article concluded:

> Nothing was mentioned of the rest of the crew, so it is assumed they remained on board their ship but through the gallantry of the Tyrella lifeboat, part at least of her crew have been saved. (ix)

Five crew were saved, but there were no further newspaper reports as to what happened to the rest of the men or the steamer, other than the fact that Shipping Records show the *Wild Rose* left Dundrum for Cardiff two weeks after the rescue.

The second 'shout' for the lifeboat ended up being the subject of a court case at the Quarter Sessions in Downpatrick. The Action was between the coxswain John Gordon, and the owner of a vessel called the *Fly*. This account was published in the *Belfast News Letter* in January 1890:

John Gordon, the plaintiff, deposed that he was coxswain of the Tyrella lifeboat on 1st

December 1889. An officer of the coastguards rapped him up between 6 and 7 o'clock and reported that there was a vessel riding at anchor outside the rocks in the Bay of Dundrum. The vessel afterwards showed a flag which led to assistance being wanted. He summoned a crew and got the lifeboat launched. He had 26 helpers and 13 of a crew. The wind was blowing south onto the shore; there were 13 men in our boat when we left for the vessel and after a while we hailed her and found her to be the *Fly* of Preston, without cargo, bound for Dundrum. The captain asked for a pilot, and so the lifeboat went through heavy seas and took in Pat Megraw through a heavy sea to the *Fly*. His claim was for 4 shillings and 6 pence each per man for the helpers and ten shillings each per man for the crew of the lifeboat; this was the rate by which the National Lifeboat Institution pay. The witness had been offered £2 and after issue of the process £5 in settlement, which he refused. After further evidence, His Lordship gave a decree of ten shillings each for the crew – a total of £6 10 shillings. (x)

Rule 19 of the Lifeboat Regulations stipulated that lifeboats should not be used to take off anchors, or stores or a pilot, or orders to a ship, except in an emergency. This was further explained by Richard Lewis:

(42) Self-righting lifeboat on slipway.

As it often happens that the lifeboats of the National Lifeboat Institution are called on to aid in saving vessels and their cargoes from destruction, whilst the owners of such property have not infrequently objected to paying the lifeboatmen for the services, (believing that they are only performing their duty by rendering them)… In the first place, it cannot be too plainly stated or too generally known that the National Lifeboat Institution is a society established for the saving of human lives and that only. It appeals to the British public to support it for that object and that object alone. It has therefore no right to devote any part of the funds so raised to providing means for saving property or for any other object other than the philanthropic one, which is its special vocation. Accordingly, it is a misapprehension on the part of the owners of property at sea to suppose that it is the duty of the men who work the Institute's lifeboats on the coast, to give their services gratuitously to effect its preservation. The Institution pays them for devoting their time and labour, and for risking their lives to save the lives of others and it has no claim on them to do more. On the other hand,…valuable property should not be allowed to perish beneath the waves if it can be saved. The Institute authorises the crews of lifeboats to assist in saving vessels stranded, or leaky, or otherwise in distress under special circumstances and on certain terms… such service, being altogether distinct from the function of the institution, it was considered expedient to separate it, as far as possible from the more legitimate employment of its boats; it was arranged that, on all occasions of using the Institute's lifeboat to save property, they were to be considered as 'lent' to their crews for that purpose, and the latter should look to the owners of the property to remunerate them in accordance with the provisions of the Merchant Shipping Act, and not the Institute. "(xi)

John Gordon's action in seeking payment from the owner of the *Fly* was only in line with the Regulations set out by the Institution; it would have been expected of him, as Coxswain of the lifeboat involved, to pursue the matter, if necessary to court, to secure payment for his crew.

The next report of the *Louisa Burnaby* was of a routine quarterly practice in September 1894.

One of these official practices takes place at night once each year, in order to keep the crew posted up, in case anything should occur in Dundrum Bay at night. This night practice, in connection with the life-saving apparatus, took place at Tyrella, under the superintendence of Messrs Gordon and Kerr. The crew is made up of the immediate inhabitants of the district. The men went through the different movements in quick style, the launch especially, which was done with remarkable speed. Day practice also takes place at given intervals, but there is more curiosity attached to the night manoeuvres. Dundrum Bay is considered one of the most dangerous places along the Co Down coast; hence the lifeboat being located there but fortunately it has not been called into requisition much. The Hon Sec., the Rev D Kennedy was in attendance. (xii)

The number of shipwrecks had decreased dramatically in the previous decade, and although Dundrum Bay still claimed the unwary and unlucky sailing ship, the era of sail had largely given way to steam power. The particular perils of being embayed if caught in a southerly or south-easterly gale was of little importance to a steam powered ship.

RNLI records show three other 'shouts' for the *Louisa Burnaby*. On 14 April 1894, the lifeboat went out in a south-easterly gale to the assistance of the *Mary Ann*, driven close to the shore at Rathmullen, but she was able to anchor, and the services of the lifeboat were not required. On the way back, the East Downshire Company's steamship, the *Lady Arthur Hill* was spotted in some difficulty crossing the bar at Dundrum to gain access to the quay. Although the lifeboat stood by, the steamship was able to enter the Inner Harbour without further assistance. In July 1895, the lifeboat went out to rescue two fishermen whose boat had capsized after it hit the Cow and Calf rocks; the two brothers had held on to the keel of the upturned boat until spotted by the coastguards at Tyrella. The sea was relatively calm and after the brothers were safe their boat was towed back in to shore at the same time by the lifeboat. The final 'shout' for the lifeboat was on Christmas Eve 1895, when it went out in a south-easterly gale and very heavy sea to a fully rigged ship that had been observed drifting close to St John's Lighthouse and was having difficulties in rounding the Point. The lifeboat succeeded in assisting the ship to anchor, so that it was able to clear the Point when the wind moderated the following day and make it safely into Killough for repairs.

The *Louisa Burnaby* had a final moment, sharing the limelight in 1898 with a lifeboat from Groomsport, Co Down, when they took part in 'Lifeboat Saturday' in Belfast "…on the occasion of a grand Royal National Lifeboat Institution Parade and fundraiser for the Northern Irish Branch of the Royal National Lifeboat Institution, held at the Waterworks, North Belfast" [The Waterworks were then still owned by the Water Board, but they had obtained a licence to use the site for leisure purposes in 1889, and had rowing boats, shortly followed by public bathing and aquatic sports. It was an ideal venue in Belfast to demonstrate life-saving and have real lifeboats on view for the Belfast public to see.] The article enumerated all the activities offered on the day, along with a detailed description of the entertainment provided and concluded: "Thanks are due to the Rev SS Holmes of Groomsport and Rev D Kennedy of Tyrella, for the very great

(43) The first Lifeboat Saturday in Manchester. There is a lifeboat on a trailer with the crew on board.

interest and trouble they took in the matter for the arrangements and for their respective crews and boats." (xiii) The sum of £1,068.2.0 was raised on the day and forwarded to the RNLI.

Charles Wright Macara was the architect of these Lifeboat Saturdays; an industrial magnate who had made his fortune from cotton-spinning factories in Manchester, he was concerned that "not more than 25,000 people out of the many millions who constituted this great maritime nation contributed to the lifeboat…" Because of this he "had an idea which brought charity into the streets and the streets into charity". This was to make direct contact between the lifeboat crews and the public of the great inland towns. It was the genesis of what were to be known as Lifeboat Saturdays. These were the forerunners of the modern flag-day.' The actual event, was in fact carried out over several days:

The whole affair was staged with imagination and after very careful planning. On Thursday and Friday two Lancashire lifeboat crews paraded cities and suburbs; they were in fact drawn from stations which had more than one lifeboat as well as an adequate reserve of volunteers. On Saturday began the serious business; lifeboat crews and bands parading, lifeboats on their carriages, detachments from fire-brigade and ambulance units. Lifeboats were actually launched in the artificial lake in Bellevue Gardens, Manchester, and in the evening a rescue by rocket apparatus was staged. This was watched by a crowd estimated at 30,000. (xiv)

The final total collection came to £5,000, a staggering sum of money for the time, with £600 being lifted in coppers dropped into boxes by the public walking by. The idea quickly spread, and in 1894 Belfast held its first Lifeboat Saturday.

An occasion, with a striking similarity to 'Lifeboat Saturday', had occurred in Dublin some 20 years earlier, in February 1871. *Saunders's News Letter* noted:

The Grand National Bazaar, in aid of the Irish auxiliary of this most valuable institution [RNLI] was opened yesterday in the Exhibition Palace and will be continued today. We are happy to say that the bazaar, concert and ball, promoted in the interests of those who brave "the perils of the deep" promise to be more than ordinarily successful… The building was thronged to excess throughout the day with a highly fashionable assembly of ladies and gentlemen and an immense and profitable business was carried on… The stalls were arranged beneath the galleries on both sides of the nave…all were gaily decorated with flags, banners and evergreens… There are now about 30 lifeboats stationed around the Irish coast. The object of the promoters of the bazaar is to increase that number if possible from the sum to be realised as profit and if possible excite the sympathy of the wealthy noblemen and gentlemen in the country to aid in the erection of stations where they are needed… amongst the ladies present were the Marchioness of Drogheda, Countess of Howth, Countess of Granard; …Lady Margaret Stronge ran the Portrush stall and Mrs Galtsmith, the Tyrella stall… In order to further advertise the existence of the bazaar, the Howth lifeboat, gaily decorated and manned with its full crew, wearing their life-belts &c was drawn on its carriage through the streets of the city and attracted no little attention. (xv)

It is clear from the account that the events were aimed at the wealthy and middle classes of Dublin, and so was typical of the appeal being made to those classes in the second half of the 19th Century. The Howth Lifeboat and crew going through the streets of Dublin would have drawn the attention of all classes to the Institution; it was an astute attention-raising ploy, but there is no indication that any monies were raised in the streets as the Lifeboat passed by.

The idea of appealing directly to the wider public was just a recognition of the social revolution that had swept across the United Kingdom; the philanthropy of the landed gentry who gave the one-off generous donations that enabled the Institution to come into being in 1824, had been supplemented by the bequests and legacies of the more modestly well-to-do in the middle of the century. By the end of the 19th Century, society was almost unrecognisable; industrialisation had created huge urban populations, the railways had encouraged both geographic and social mobility, and the working class had begun to claim its rights in social care, the right to vote and the right to be educated. The Royal National Lifeboat Institution needed to secure the support now of the wider public and so Lifeboat Saturdays became the prime vehicle for doing so.

The appearance of the Tyrella lifeboat at the 2nd Belfast Lifeboat Saturday in 1898 was its swansong. In October 1899 the Institution made the decision to close the Station and sell off the Boat House.

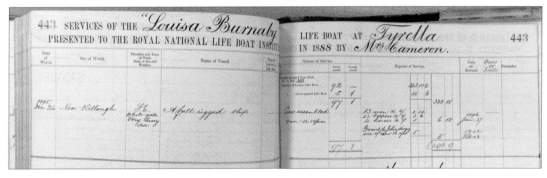

(44) Final entry in the Service Book for Tyrella Station 1895.

Chapter 8:
Epitaph

The Lifeboat at Tyrella station has been removed and the station closed. The committee of management of the RNLI have arranged to establish a station at Rossglass, adjoining St John's Point, thinking it a more suitable place for speedily launching the lifeboat and proceeding to the relief of vessels and their crews in case of need. (i)

The actual decision was to establish the Branch at Killough, but to have the boat sited at Rossglass, it being on the North-Eastern end of Dundrum Bay, rather than the lifeboat having to get from Killough, and round St John's Point, before it could approach any vessel in distress in Dundrum Bay. The new Boat House was only a short distance from where the 1825 boat house had been sited. A meeting was held in Killough in November 1899 to establish the new Branch and set up a local Committee, as was the requirement of the National Lifeboat Institution. The reports of the meeting in the local press indicated clearly a great sense of pride amongst the people of Killough, especially the merchants and fishermen, in having been chosen as the site of the new Branch. There was a delay in getting a lease for the new Boat House and so, despite the Branch coming into existence formally in 1901, it was not until 1904 that a boat arrived. The *John Groome* remained until Killough Station was closed in 1914. During the period 1899–1904 the Newcastle boat, *The Farnley*, had to cover the whole of Dundrum Bay, a task that would have been impossible had it not been for the diminishing number of vessels needing help. The few wrecks in the Bay in the first decade of the 20th century were all sailing ships, the in-draught in Dundrum Bay that caused so much problem to sailing ships being of minimal concern to a steamship.

So little was said in the local press in 1899 about the closure of the Tyrella Station, it was almost as if the Tyrella Branch of the RNLI had never existed. However, the writing had been on the wall for the station for a number of years as the RNLI Inspector's Reports show. Concern had first been voiced in the 1870's about the loss of the best boatmen because quite a few local fishermen had emigrated, and this trend continued through to the 1890's. Where once the fishermen's cottages had lined the Clanmaghery shoreline, by the end of the 19th century a number lay empty and the men left no longer engaged in fishing but working as farm labourers. The Coxswain, John Gordon and the Assistant Coxswain, William Kerr were the only experienced boatmen left on the crew and they were both in their 60's, having served well

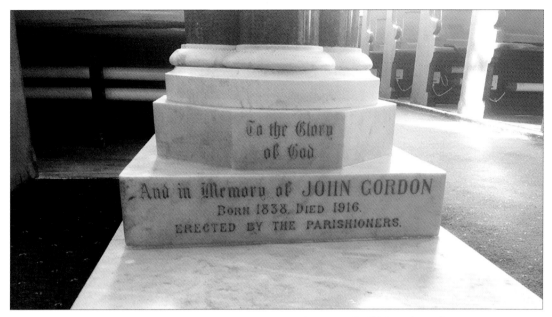

To the Glory
of God

And in Memory of JOHN GORDON
BORN 1838. DIED 1916.
ERECTED BY THE PARISHIONERS.

(45) Font engraved in memory of the former Coxswain of the Tyrella lifeboat John Gordon.

over 25 years each on the Tyrella lifeboats. Both were given an annual RNLI pension when the station was closed; the parishioners of St John's, Tyrella subscribed to a beautiful marble font in honour of John Gordon, which sits just underneath the memorial plaque to the Rev TF Martin.

The years had also taken their toll on the once handsome and well-built Boat House; its isolated site had been ideally suited for rescue in the days of sail, being built half-way between Dundrum Bar and St John's Point. Standing at the edge of a field, just a little beyond the highest tide levels, it was on a very exposed sandy beach, which would have given it little shelter from the biting easterly winds. In 1895 both the RNLI Engineer and the Architect reported that it was not worth doing major structural repairs to it, although they authorised some minor work.

For the National Lifeboat Institution, the biggest problem was:

> …that this Branch had only three members of Committee, two of whom live at some
> distance from the station. There is virtually no Committee and no material from which
> to form one. (ii)

Like the dearth of experienced boatmen for crew, the 'material from which' a Committee could be formed had been decreasing over the latter years of the 19th century. The era of the local

(46) Tyrella Lifeboat House, perched on edge of field, in a snowstorm (2018).

landed gentry and 'Big Houses' had ended; many of the grand houses by 1899 were lying empty and soon to become derelict. Others had passed through multiple different tenants and owners, some becoming summer residences. Tyrella House had finally ended up being purchased by James Craig, who had made his fortune in trade; he bought it as a summer residence to escape out of Belfast and was a very well-liked and respected country squire for the time that he spent there. The Craig family, were well known for their involvement in Unionist politics (Craig's son Lord Craigavon was the first Unionist prime-minister of Northern Ireland) but while James Craig was a benevolent landlord, he took little or no interest in the lifeboat. There were no longer horses all year in the Tyrella stables that could be used to haul the carriage, and other arrangements with a local farmer had to be set in place. The natural leadership of the resident gentry who had been involved in all matters local, had gone. The Hon Secretary of the Branch, the Rev David Kennedy, no longer just tended to the needs of the parishioners of Tyrella, but also assisted with those of Rathmullen and Bright, the Church of Ireland population in the area having dwindled so much in the latter years of the 19th century that the upkeep of these as separate parishes was no longer viable. So, where Rev Martin could devote time to the lifeboat cause and be an active Hon Secretary, the Rev Kennedy had much less time to spare for non-parochial business.

RNLI minutes show that the preference of the National Committee for Killough as the site for the new Branch was largely based on the availability of a good number of fishermen to man the boats, and the willingness of its merchants and citizens to form a Branch Committee. These were the very attributes that Tyrella had enjoyed in 1860, but had lost by the end of the century, due to the de-population of the area. With only scattered farms and transient farm labourers, there was little sense of community and without a community the station could not survive. Just over ten years later the Tyrella Coastguard Station was decommissioned and the last link with the Tyrella lifeboats ended. It is not surprising that there is no folk-memory, no plaques or memorials, no mention in local history books or on neighbouring RNLI website histories.

The Lifeboat (January 1861) noted:

> A lifeboat station has been established at Tyrella on the north side of Dundrum Bay… it is anticipated that this lifeboat will be of much service on this exposed part of the coast. (iii)

It could be said that this small station exceeded expectations. Out of the forty-eight lifeboat stations in Ireland at this time, only seven lifeboat stations saved more people (see table in Appendix 7)… a proud record for an isolated and wind-swept station.

A fitting epitaph for the brave men who manned the Forgotten Lifeboats of Tyrella can be found in a speech made by the Admiral of the Fleet, Sir George Sartorius KCB in 1876:

> Everything done had been done by volunteers, for the brave lifeboat crews were all volunteers. The perils of night, of wind and cold, the launching of the boat, were difficulties of which those living at home at ease had but slight notion; few knew the pluck required for such work. (iv)

Warriors of the Sea

'When in dark nights of winter,
Fierce storms of wind and rain
Howl round the cosy homestead
And lash the windowpane;
When over hill and tree-top
We hear the Tempests roar
And hurricanes go sweeping on
From valley to the shore.
When nature seems to stand at bay
And silent terror comes
And those we love on earth the best
Are gathered in our homes.
Think of the sailors round the coast,
Who, braving sleet or snow,
Leave sweethearts, wives and little ones
When duty bids them go!
Think of our sea-girt island!
A harbour where alone
No lifeboatman to save a life
Has failed to risk his own.
Then when the storm howls loudest
Pray of your charity
That God will bless the lifeboat,
And the Warriors of the Sea.'

Extract from the poem Warriors of the Sea, written by Clement Scott 1886, in memory of the lifeboat crews of Southport and St Anne's lost 9 December 1886, in trying to rescue the ship Mexico.

Quoted in Frank Mundell (1894) p31

Appendix 1
Ships wrecked or aground from Dundrum Bar to St John's Point 1747–1897

(Based on information from contemporary newspapers, *Lloyd's Lists* and RNLI Archives)

Date	Name	Route	Type	Cargo	Location	Fate
05.02.1747	*Sarah*	Liverpool – West Indies			Dundrum Bay	Ran ashore
09.02.1747	*Swarthe*	Liverpool – Tortula (West Indies)			Dundrum Bay	Stranded
	Success	Plymouth – Dublin		Passengers	St John's Point	Wrecked; 29 perished
08.12.1749	*Ranger*	Londonderry – Streights		Part of it saved	Dundrum Bay	Wreck
13.03 1753	*John Daniel*	London – Coleraine	Sloop	Iron & flour	Dundrum Bay	Wrecked; cargo lost
05.02.1765	*Lady Agnetta*	Rotterdam – Dublin	Dutch	Mostly destroyed	Dundrum Bay	Wrecked
19.10.1777	*Peggy*	Liverpool – Belfast	Sloop		Craigalea, Tyrella	Cargo safe
02.01.1784	*Liverpool*	London – Londonderry	Brig (250 tons)		Clanmaghery	Crew & part of cargo safe; ship wrecked
30.04.1785	*Isabella*	Cowes – Belfast	Brigantine	Wheat	Dundrum Bay	Driven ashore, cargo lost, ship wrecked
02.01.1788	*New Loyalty*	Liverpool – Belfast	Sloop (70 tons)	Sugar wool cloth	Tyrella	Stranded
23.03.1789	*James*	Dublin – Coleraine		General cargo	Dundrum Bar	Wrecked; all crew perished
10.04.1789	*Jennet*	Dublin – Belfast	Sloop		Dundrum Bay	Wrecked; all hands lost
06.09.1795	Unknown	Isle of Man – Portsmouth	Transport Vessel	150 troops	Dundrum Bay	Stranded; troops safe

Date	Name	Route	Type	Cargo	Location	Fate
25.01.1804	*Carolina*	Dublin – Aberdeen	Brig	Ballast	Dundrum Bay	Crew safe; ship destroyed
05.06.1804	*William*	Liverpool – Newfoundland	Brig	Salt	Tyrella	Grounded; re-floated.
05.06.1804	*Castor*	Jamaica – Liverpool	Ship	Cotton, rum sugar	Tyrella	Driven ashore, got off;
03.03.1807	*Ann*	Liverpool – Glasgow			Tyrella	Total wreck; all crew lost
26.08.1807	*Satisfaction*	Liverpool – Pictou (Nova Scotia)		General cargo	Dundrum Bay	Vessel wrecked, cargo lost
29.10.1807	*Fame*	Dublin – Galway	Sloop	Port wine	St John's Point	Stranded; auction of wine
26.12.1808	*Lune*	Liverpool – Strangford	Brig	Coal	Tyrella	Cargo lost; ship safe
26.12.1808	*Providence*	Liverpool – Coleraine	Sloop	Sugar, salt	Tyrella	3 crew safe; vessel wrecked
10.09.1809	*Lion*	Dublin – Belfast – Quebec	Brig		Tyrella	On shore; much damage
04.02.1810	*Lottery*	Liverpool – New Providence	Ship	Porter, brick	Dundrum Bay	Crew safe; ship wrecked
16.02.1810	*Elizabeth*	Jamaica – Liverpool	Barque	Rum, cotton	Dundrum Bay	Total wreck, all crew lost
03.04.1810	*Britannia*	Cork – Liverpool			Ballyvaston	Grounded; re-floated
14.11.1810	*Molly*	Dublin – Newry		Passengers	Dundrum Bay	3 saved, 10 lost, ship wrecked
18.01.1811	*Emelia*	Philadelphia – Liverpool	Ship	Cotton, logwood	Craigalea, Tyrella	Wrecked; crew of 14 saved
05.02.1811	*Thomas*	Liverpool – Tobermorey	Sloop	Coal, oil, tar, butter	Ballyvaston	Wrecked in 10 minutes; crew saved
10.01.1814	*John & Sarah*	Strangford – Dublin	Sloop (27 tons)		Tyrella	Wrecked; all aboard lost
10.01 1814	Fishing Fleet	Out of Annalong	Fishing smack		Dundrum Bay	4 boats lost; 27 dead
25.02.1814	*Mary*	Biboa – Belfast			Dundrum Bay	Driven onshore; got off

Date	Name	Route	Type	Cargo	Location	Fate
11.12.1814	*Auspicious*	Liverpool – Newry			Dundrum Bay	Wrecked
23.10.1815	*Cherub*	Liverpool – Belfast – Jamaica			Dundrum Bay	Stranded; refloated
23.10.1815	*Mary*	Sicily – Belfast			Dundrum Bay	Driven onshore; got off
06.10.1818	*Ruby*	Liverpool – Newry			Dundrum Bay	Total wreck; all hands lost
12.11.1818	*Minerva*	Liverpool – Belfast		Coal	Dundrum Bar	Ran aground; got off with cargo
15.01.1819	*Messmate*	Liverpool – Killough	Schooner (75 tons)	Coal	Dundrum Bay	Ran aground; wrecked.
15.01 1819	*Louisa*	Liverpool – Killough	Schooner	Coal	Dundrum Bar	Total wreck; crew lost
20.01.1820	*The Lady Montgomery*	Irvine – Dublin			Dundrum Bay	Total wreck
24.01.1820	*Collins*	Canada – Liverpool	Brig		Tyrella	Wrecked
27.09.1820	*Hardwicke*	Chasing smuggler	Revenue cutter		Cow & Calf, Tyrella	Crew saved; ship wrecked
12.02.1822	*Aurora*	Liverpool – Dundalk	Brig (131 tons)		Rathmullan	Ran ashore; auctioned on site
10.02.1823	*Provestein*	Denmark – Dublin		Timber, plank	Dundrum Bay	Wrecked; cargo saved
10.02.1823	*Belvoir Castle*	Dublin – Whitehaven			Dundrum Bay	Grounded; got off
10.02.1823	*Henry*	Whitehaven – Dublin			Dundrum Bay	Total wreck
10.02.1823	*Ann*	Whitehaven – Strangford			Dundrum Bay	Driven ashore
17.03 1825	*John Little*	Liverpool – Halifax	Barque	Salt	Rossglass	Wrecked; 13 crew dead, 2 saved
18.03 1825	*Catherine*	Workington – Dundalk	100 tons	Coal	Craigalea, Tyrella	Wrecked; 6 crew saved
12.09.1825	*Superior*	Liverpool – New York	American ship		Tyrella	Stranded & wrecked
08.10.1825	*Hopewell*	Greenock – Limerick	Brig	Ballast	Ballyvaston	Wrecked; crew safe

Date	Name	Route	Type	Cargo	Location	Fate
15.11.1825	*Usk*	Liverpool – Adra, Spain	Brig (105 tons)	Coal	Rossglass	5 crew lost; 2 saved
06.03.1826	*Richard Pope*	Liverpool – Sierra Leone	Barque		Dundrum Bay	Wrecked; crew drowned
07.03.1827	*Mary*	Liverpool – Dublin	Sloop		Dundrum Bay	Driven ashore; 4 crew lost
16.11.1827	*Catherine*	Liverpool – Killough	Sloop		Craigalea, Tyrella	Stranded; 4 saved lifeboat
28.11.1827	*Blue-Eyed Maid*	Liverpool – Tyne			Dundrum Bay	Driven ashore; got off
02.04.1828	*Hope*	Newport – Glasgow	Sloop		Ballyvaston	Run aground; got off
02.04.1828	*Elizabeth*	From Workington	Schooner	Coal	Ballyvaston	Bilged & wrecked; auction on site
03.12.1829	*Sir James Kempt*	Canada – Liverpool	Ship	Timber	Tyrella	Wrecked; 13 saved
16.03.1830	*Sally*	Maryport – Dublin			Tyrella	Total wreck; crew lost
02.10.1830	*Pelorus*	Liverpool – Lisbon	Brig		Tyrella	Driven ashore; refloated
10.11.1830	*Ann*	Newport Aberdeen		Iron	Dundrum Bay	Driven ashore; total wreck
16.11.1830	*Mary*	Whitehaven – Dublin		Iron, coal	Dundrum Bay	Driven ashore
17.12.1831	*Brothers*	Dublin – Wick	Sloop	Ballast	Dundrum Bay	Bilged & wrecked; crew safe
06.01.1832	*New Diligence*	Cardiff – Newry	Sloop	Iron	Dundrum Bay	Driven ashore; crew safe
21.03.1832	*Westmoreland*	Portrush – Liverpool	Sloop	Butter oatmeal	Dundrum Bar	Wrecked; crew lost
05.08.1832	*Delafore*	Liverpool – Quebec	Barque	Ballast	Tyrella	Stranded; re-floated
25.12.1832	*Catherine* (of Campbelton)	From Liverpool		Iron & salt	Dundrum Bay	Driven ashore; re-floated
29.12.1832	*Catherine*	Bangor, Wales – Newry			Dundrum Bay	Driven ashore
18.12.1833	*Earl of Aberdeen*	Quebec – Belfast	Brig	Timber	Dundrum Bay	Driven ashore; re-floated

Date	Name	Route	Type	Cargo	Location	Fate
25.12.1833	*Wesley*	Onega, Russia – Bristol			Dundrum Bay	Driven ashore; re-floated
02.05.1834	*Alpha*	Dublin – Ballywalter	Sloop		Tyrella	Aground; got off
05.11.1834	*Aid*	Conway, Wales – Sunderland	Schooner	Slates	Tyrella	Wrecked; crew safe
14.03.1835	*Heroine*	Liverpool – New Orleans	Ship (353 tons)	Salt & earthenware	Tyrella	Wrecked
13.09.1835	*Diligence*	Wales to Newry	Sloop	Slates	Dundrum Bay	Onshore; re-floated
06.11.1835	*Charlotte*	Glasgow – Drogheda	Sloop (60 tons)		Tyrella	Wrecked; 5 lost
14.11.1835	*Janet*		Sloop		Dundrum Bay	Stranded; re-floated
13.12.1836	*Menapia*	From Waterford	Schooner (164 tons)		St John's Point	Total wreck; 5 crew lost
1836	*Margaret*	From Liverpool	Sloop	Coal	Dundrum Bay	Total wreck; 4 lost
11.09.1837	*Coeur de Lion*	Liverpool – Quebec	Ship (600 tons)	General cargo	Tyrella	Wrecked; 7 lost
23.09.1837	*Henry Bowers*	Liverpool – Belfast			Tyrella	Driven ashore; re-floated
02.12.1837	*Jane*	From Portaferry	Sloop		Tyrella	2 crew lost
16.12.1837	*George*	Swansea – Liverpool			Dundrum Bay	Driven ashore; sank
13.01.1838	*London*	From Plymouth	Schooner	General cargo	Dundrum Bar	wrecked
21.01.1838	*Union*	Whitehaven – Drogheda	Schooner	Coal	Tyrella	Wrecked; 6 crew saved
23.02.1838	*Constitution*	Liverpool – Charleston	Ship		Near St John's Pt	Total wreck; crew safe
22.10 1838	*Bloom*	Bangor, Wales – Dysart	Schooner	Slates	St John's Pt	Total wreck; 3 safe, 3 lost
23.10.1838	*Rapid*	Bangor, Wales – Londondery	Schooner	Ballast	Tyrella	Stranded; 3 lost
23.10 1838	*Stranger*	Liverpool – Londonderry	Brig	Salt	Tyrella	Total wreck; crew lost
23.10 1838	*Friendship*	Bangor, Wales – Berwick	Schooner	Slates	Tyrella	Total wreck; crew safe

Date	Name	Route	Type	Cargo	Location	Fate
29.11.1838	*British Heroine*	Liverpool to Mobile, USA	Ship (610 tons)	Salt	Tyrella	20 saved by Tyrella lifeboat
19.02.1839	*Active*	Liverpool – Belfast	Schooner	General Cargo	Ballyvaston	Stranded; 5 crew safe
06.08.1839	*Emily*	From Belfast	Schooner		Rossglass	Wrecked; all crew lost
10.08.1839	*Archibald*	Belfast – Neath (Wales)	Schooner	Sand ballast	Rossglass	Wreck
11.08.1839	Unknown	From Belfast	Schooner		Tyrella	Total wreck
17.08.1839	*Albert*	Belfast – Wexford	Schooner		St John's Point	Ashore on rocks; got off
12.01.1840	*Eagle*	Liverpool – Newcastle Tyne	Schooner	Rock salt	Rossglass	Crew of 8 safe; auction on site
18.01.1840	*Trevor*	Alicante – Belfast	Brig (162 tons)	Brimstone (sulphur)	Tyrella	Wreck; crew safe- Lifeboat
18.01.1840	*Kincardineshire*	Liverpool – Aberdeen	Brig	Cotton, lead, iron, salt	Tyrella	Stranded; crew safe
26.09.1840	*Sarah*		Smack	Copper bolts & sheets	St John's Point	Wrecked
12.01.1841	*Philestrius*	New Orleans – Greenock	Brig	Cotton	Dundrum Bay	Wreck; 20 dead, 3 safe
22.01.1842	*Zephyr*	From Liverpool	Schooner		Dundrum Bar	Stranded; got off
24.01.1842	*Oliver Boyd*	Bangor, Wales – Glasgow	Smack	Slates	Clanmaghery	Stranded; auction slates
13.01.1843	Fishing fleet of 16 boats	Newcastle & Annalong	Fishing smacks		Dundrum Bay	11 boats lost; 73 dead
08.03.1844	*Industry*	Aberdovey – Strangford	Sloop	Bark	Rathmullan	Grounded; re-floated
09.03.1844	*Peace & Plenty*	Drogheda – Inverness	Smack		Rossglass	Ashore; got off
05.06.1844	*Kitty*	Liverpool – Quebec			Dundrum Bay	Ashore; refloated
17.01.1845	*Frolic*	Liverpool – Dordt, Holland	Schooner		Dundrum Bar	Total wreck; 6 rescued
13.09.1845	*Industry*	Belfast – North Africa	Brig (145 tons)		Minerstown	Wrecked; 8 crew safe

Date	Name	Route	Type	Cargo	Location	Fate
02.12.1845	*Active*		Brig		Dundrum Bay	Wrecked; crew safe
22.12 1845	*Gloom*		Brig		Dundrum Bay	Wrecked; crew safe
22.12.1845	*Gloria*	Liverpool – Stettin (Poland)	Brig	Palm Oil, soda ash	St John's Point	All crew saved
23.09.1846	*Great Britain*	Liverpool – New York	Iron steamship	Passengers	Dundrum Bay	Grounded; 11 months to be refloated
17.12.1847	*Ida*	Runcorn – Newry	Schooner	Rock salt	Tyrella	Capsized 6 crew lost
17.12.1847	*Lowther*	Cardiff – Ross	Schooner	Coal	Tyrella	Crew saved by lifeboat
20.03.1849	*Rover*	Liverpool – Strangford	Schooner	Railway iron & slates	St John's Point	Vessel & crew saved
09.08.1849	*Gypsy*	Chepstow – Clyde	Ketch	Oak planks for navy	Dundrum Bay	Ashore; refloated
06.04.1850	*Sarah Ann*	Liverpool to Canada	Barque	Ballast	Tyrella	Crew saved by lifeboat
01.11.1850	*San Antonio*	Cork – Troon	Brig (250 tons)	Ballast	Minerstown	Crew safe; refloated
20.11.1850	*Welcome*	Fleetwood – Newry	Brigantine	Coals	Craigalea, Tyrella	Stranded; refloated
14.12.1850	Unknown	Out of Annalong	Fishing smack		Dundrum Bay	Capsized; 6 lost
29.09.1851	*Orford*	Workington – Dublin	Brig (130 tons)	Coal	Minerstown	Wrecked; crew safe
12.02.1852	*Juliana*	Carnarvon – Ayr	Sloop	Slates	Dundrum Bay	Crew & cargo safe
12.11.1852	*Martha Grace*	Maryport – Dublin	Schooner (62 tons)	Coal	Dundrum Bar	3 crew rescued
19.01.1853	*Lord Ashburton*	Liverpool – New Orleans	Sloop (1000 tons)		Rossglass	Stranded
23.07.1853	Unknown	Belfast – Dublin	Yacht		Dundrum Bay	Fishermen rescued crew
09.11.1853	*Victoria*	Dublin – Belfast			Dundrum Bay	Ran ashore; got off
21.01.1854	*Catherine Corrigan*	Cardiff – Cork	Schooner	Coal	Hit Cow & Calf rocks	Crew lost; ship wrecked
27.01 1854	*Lively*	From Preston	Schooner	Coal	Dundrum Bay	Total wreck; crew lost

Date	Name	Route	Type	Cargo	Location	Fate
03.02.1854	*John O'Gaunt*	From the Americas	Ship	Cotton bales	Rossglass	Wrecked
03.03.1854	*Charles Humberston*	Liverpool – Boston USA	Full rigger (1100 tons)	Passengers & cargo	Tyrella	Wreck; failed to get off
11.06.1854	*Sea Bird*	Dublin – Ardrossan	Brig	Ballast	St John's Point	Ashore; crew safe
28.10.1854	*Jupiter*	Liverpool – Vera Cruz	Barque (214 tons)	Coal	Tyrella	Wreck; 10 crew safe
28.10.1854	Unknown	From Dundee		General merchandise	Dundrum Bay	Ship and crew all lost
05.01.1855	Fishing boat	Out of Raymonde	Fishing smack		Tyrella	Wreck; 4 crew dead
06.01.1855	*Atalanta*	For Newry	Sloop	Coal	Hit Cow & Calf rocks	Crew of 4 drowned
14.10.1855	*Marie-Raymonde*	Bordeaux – Glasgow	Square rigged	Flour, brandy	Dundrum Bay	Stranded; refloated
17.05.1855	*Fortune*	Liverpool – Hobart	Barque (571 tons)	Cargo + 233 passengers	Craigalea Tyrella	Stranded; 1 crew lost
04.04.1856	*Nautilis*	Dundalk – Killough	Smack (33 tons)	Oatmeal	St John's Point	Wrecked; crew safe
07.01.1857	*Fingalton*	Liverpool – Newcastle Tyne	Barque (860 tons)	Salt	Pladdy rocks Tyrella	Stranded; towed off
15.09.1857	*James Gibbs*	Quebec – Glasgow		Timber	St John's Point	Stranded; towed off
07.04.1858	*John Duncan*	Savannah – Liverpool	Brig	Rice, sugar	Tyrella	Driven ashore; refloated
07.04.1858	*Prude*	Wales to Irvine	Sloop	Bark	Rossglass	Driven ashore; crew safe
08.04.1858	*War Cloud*	Calcutta – Liverpool	East Indiaman	Tea, general cargo	Rossglass	Anchored; tugs got off
18.12.1858	*Louise Amelie*	Out of Nantes	Lugger		Tyrella	Crew of 5 saved
04.12.1859	*Tiky*	Odessa – Glasgow	Brig (400 tons)	Bagged grain	Cow & Calf Tyrella	6 dead & 9 saved
18.10 1860	*Martha Whitmore*	Richmond USA – Glasgow	Ship (700 tons)	Wheat & flour	St John's Point	Anchored; lifeboat went
12.06.1861	*John Bull*	Liverpool – Quebec	Barque	Cargo & 14 passengers	Rossglass	Lifeboat assist in mooring

Date	Name	Route	Type	Cargo	Location	Fate
27.09.1861	*Glasgow*	Wick – Waterford	Schooner (99 tons)	Herring	Rossglass	Wreck; crew safe – lifeboat
11.01.1862	*Solferino*	Dublin – Ardrossan	Schooner (89 tons)	Ballast	Rathmullen	Total wreck; lifeboat
17.01.1862	*Bellona*	Liverpool – Dundrum	Schooner (55 tons)	Coal	Dundrum Bay	Wreck; 1 crew safe – lifeboat
16.10.1862	*Tickler*	Howth – Ardglass	Smack	Herring	Rathmullen	Wreck; all lost
02.01.1864	*Hamilton Gray*	Liverpool – Spezzia (Italy)	Barque (567 tons)	Coal	Dundrum Bar	Crew safe; ship wrecked
14.09.1864	*Sarah*	Ardrossan – Newport	Schooner (110 tons)	Pig iron	St John's Point	Sank; crew in own boat
18.11.1864	*Rook*	Liverpool – Newry	Schooner	Coal	Minerstown	Went ashore
18.11.1864	*Cottager*	Maryport – Kingstown	Brigantine	Coal	Rossglass	Stranded; auction
07.02.1865	*Joseph*	Liverpool – Dundalk	Schooner	Coal	Tyrella	Stranded; refloated
06.12.1865	*Daniel O'Connell*	Liverpool – Newry	Schooner	Indian Corn	Tyrella	5 crew safe – lifeboat
12.01.1866	*Venture*	Liverpool – Dundrum	Brigantine	Coal	Tyrella	Ashore; refloated
25.03.1866	*Charlotte*	Dunkirk - Londonderry	Schooner	Wheat	Rossglass	Ashore; towed off
24.03.1867	*William of Paimpol*	Bound for Iceland	Brigantine	Salt, gear for cod fishing	Tyrella	Wrecked; 6 crew safe lifeboat
19.04.1867	*Charlotte Harrison*	Liverpool – Canada	Barque	General cargo	Near St John's Point	Lifeboat assist anchoring
06.02.1870	*Eliza*	From Liverpool	Brigantine		Tyrella	Lifeboat out; not needed
02.01.1871	*Colima*	Liverpool – Guatemala	Barque (227 tons)	Linen drills	Dundrum Bar	Wrecked; crew – lifeboat
04.03.1871	*William*	To Londonderry	Brigantine		Tyrella	Grounded; 5 crew safe
09.03.1871	*Isabella*	Dublin – Portaferry	Schooner	Draff	Rathmullen	Grounded; refloated
16.08.1872	*Neptunus*	Liverpool – Copenhagen	Barque (627 tons)	Ballast	Tyrella	Wreck; 14 crew safe lifeboat

Date	Name	Route	Type	Cargo	Location	Fate
13.08.1874	*Rata*	Maryport – Belfast	Schooner	Coal	Dundrum Bay	Wrecked
26.09.1874	*Ellesmere*		Schooner		Dundrum Bay	Lost; crew ashore
29.11.1874	*Donna Maria*	Liverpool – Belfast	Brigantine (137 tons)	Timber for H & Wolff	Ballyvaston	Lifeboat saved 6
30.11.1874	Unknown	For Whitehaven		Ballast	Dundrum Bay	Capsized 3 safe-lifeboat
10.12.1874	*James*	Drogheda – Swansea	Brigantine		Dundrum Bay	Wrecked
23.02.1875	*Jura*	Dublin – Dundrum		Bone marrow	Dundrum Bar	Sails lost; driven ashore
26.02.1875	*Friends*	Girvan – Killough	Schooner	Coal	Tyrella	Crew of 4 safe-lifeboat
19.10.1875	*Lizzie*	Swansea – Belfast	Steam schooner	Coal	Ballyvaston	Beached; crew – lifeboat
02.01.1876	*Ellen*	Newry – Bangor (Down)	Schooner (61 tons)	Ballast	Black Rock, Rathmullen	Stranded
15.11.1876	*Aulini Sinai*	Nantes – Preston	Brig (149 tons)	Bagged grain	Rathmullen	Wreck; 6 crew – lifeboat
20.02.1877	*Earl*	Ardrossan – Newry			Dundrum Bay	Embayed; towed out
09.04.1877	*Ocean Packet No 3*	Out of Harlingen	Packet ship		Tyrella	Lifeboat found abandoned
13.04.1878	*Cygnet*	Silloth – Dundalk	Brigantine (118 tons)	Coal	Tyrella	Wreck; 4 crew safe – lifeboat
22.09.1878	*Wasp*	Troon – Newry	Smack (30 tons)	Coal	Tyrella	Wreck; 3 crew safe – lifeboat
02.07.1879	*Maria Brockleman*	Drogheda – Troon	Brigantine		Dundrum Bay	Needed pilot
05.11.1880	*Olaf Kyrie*		Brig		St John's Point	Lifeboat assist in rounding Pt
07.02.1881	*Bransty*	Newry – Bristol	Brigantine (80 tons)	Oats	Long Rocks, Tyrella	Wreck; 4 crew safe – lifeboat
20.04.1881	*Alfred Rooker*	Bristol – Dublin	Smack		Dundrum Bay	Ashore; got off
29.09.1881	*Gertrude*	Quebec – Belfast	Barque (949 tons)	Timber for H & Wolff	Tyrella	Stranded; 13 safe – lifeboat

Date	Name	Route	Type	Cargo	Location	Fate
13.12.1882	*Anglian*	Rotterdam – Belfast			Dundrum Bay	Grounded; got off
14.08.1883	*Henry*	Liverpool – Canada	Ship	Coal & salt	Rossglass	Anchored; 5 locals – lifeboat
09.02.1884	*Victoria*	From North Wales	Schooner (53 tons)	Slates	Minerstown	Wrecked; crew lost- lifeboat
21.01.1885	*Mary Helen*	Swansea – Dundrum	Brigantine (163 tons)	Coal	Dundrum Bar	Wreck; crew safe
21.02.1885	*Helen* (of Leith)	Liverpool – Rostrevor	Schooner (73 tons)	Coal	Tyrella	Wreck; 5 crew safe – lifeboat
18.03.1885	*Star of the West*	Waterford – Belfast	Schooner	Manure	Tyrella	Driven ashore; refloated
08.08.1885	*Rambler*	Carlingford – Liverpool	Schooner (57 tons)	Paving stones	Tyrella	Wreck; 4 crew safe – lifeboat
27.02.1886	*Barclay*	London – Ayr	Schooner (90 tons)	Manure	Smith's Rock, Tyrella	Wreck; 7 crew safe – lifeboat
24.01.1887	*Esperance*	Bangkok – Belfast	Barque (281 tons)	Teak	Smith's Rock, Tyrella	Wreck 10 crew safe – lifeboat
15.06.1887	*Hastings*	Dublin – Troon		Ballast	Dundrum Bay	Grounded; refloated
18.06.1887	*Primrose*	To Belfast	Steam yacht		Rossglass	Stranded; refloated
13.11 1888	*Wild Rose*	Donaghadee – Cardiff	Steamship		Tyrella	Lifeboat saved 5 crew
19.08.1889	*Fly*	Preston – Dundrum	Schooner (60 tons)	Ballast	Dundrum Bar	Lifeboat got pilot
14.04.1894	*Mary Ann*	Dublin – Portaferry	Schooner		Minerstown	Grounded; towed off
12.07.1895	Fishing boat	Out of Rossglass	Fishing boat		Cow & Calf Tyrella	Capsized; 2 safe – lifeboat
24.12.1895	Unknown	Heading to Killough	Full rigged ship		St John's Point	Lifeboat assisted to round Point
07.08.1897	*Raith*	Newry – Dundrum	Steamer	General cargo	Dundrum Bar	Grounded; refloated

Appendix 2
Sailing ships of the period 1747–1897

The Ships and their Rigging

The Rig refers to the masts and sails that a ship carried; the identification of the sailing ships of the period was based on the number of masts a ship carried and how they were rigged.

Masts

The mast was supported by stays (ropes) and shrouds (rigging of rope that held the mast from side to side); the shrouds also served as ladders to permit the crew to climb aloft. Until the early 19th century most masts were made from wood made from a single timber (usually the trunk of a conifer). In order to get the necessary height as ships and their masts got larger, masts were then built from several pieces of timber (known from the deck up as: Lower, Top, Topgallant and Royal).

The rigging was very intricate on fully rigged ships with literally miles of rope, and spars, requiring sailors to go aloft to move the yards or furl the sails. There were no safety harnesses and if a sailor lost his footing and fell, it is unlikely he would live to tell the tale. The mainmast is usually where any look-outs would have been posted.

Sailing vessels could have between one to four masts. The mast closest to the bow was called the **foremast**; the 2nd mast was usually the **mainmast**, and the mast closest to the stern was known as the **mizzenmast**. Originally the term **ship** referred to a 'ship-rigged' vessel, one that had three or more masts, all square-rigged. Other vessels were named according to their configuration of masts and sails… thus Barque, Brig, Brigantine, Ketch, Schooner and Sloop. There was even a difference between a 'ship' and a 'full-rigged ship'. By the end of the Age of Sail and the introduction of steam power (mid-late 19th century) it had become commonplace to refer to any sailing vessel as a 'ship'.

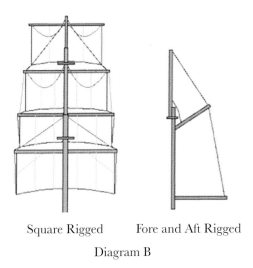

Square Rigged   Fore and Aft Rigged

Diagram B

Sails

There were two basic kinds of rigging: Square Rigged Sails & Fore and Aft Sails

Square Rigged: Sails were made of canvas, rectangular in shape and were set/hung from a horizontal spar, called a **Yard**. This was attached at the midpoint of the mast (as in the diagram above). Square rigged sails needed more men aloft to move the yards if the wind changed direction. For that reason, square rigged sails were mostly used on larger ships with a big crew, mostly on long ocean voyages where wind direction didn't vary so much, and they could use the Trade Winds to help them. A Full Rigged Ship could have as many as four masts, all square rigged, with up to five sails on each mast. The sails were also named from the deck upwards: Course, Topsail, Topgallant, Royal and Sky.

Fore and Aft Rigged: Sails were also made of canvas, that were both triangular and four sided in shape. The long edge of the mainsail was attached to the mast and the lower edge of the sail attached to a pole called the **boom**. This was hinged at the foot of the mast. The top of the sail was secured to another pole, the **gaff**. Sometimes there would be a topside sail, attached above the gaff mainsail (as shown in the diagram above.)

Fore and aft rigging was much easier to adjust than square rigging when a vessel needed to respond to wind changes; this was because sailors could work the sails from the deck by halyards and didn't have to go aloft. A smaller crew, therefore, was needed on ships that were fore and aft rigged. These kinds of ships usually sailed in coastal waters where changes in wind direction were much more common than on the deep-sea routes.

Combination Rigging: A number of vessels carried both square and fore & aft rigging. In some ships the mizzen mast was fore and aft rigged while the foremast and mainmast were square rigged. The hybrid arrangement was to allow bigger ships more manoeuvrability in the coastal trade or short sea voyages, whilst retaining the speed and stability which the square rigging gave for longer ocean voyages.

Headsails: Any sail forward of the foremast is called a headsail; this includes jibs and staysails. Jibs were triangular shaped sails attached by stays from the foremast to the **bowsprit** (a large spar which projected over the bow and on which the jib stays were anchored.) Some ships carried up to four jibs.....(Flying jib, outer and inner jib and the staysail) They gave the ship more manoeuvrability; more jibs meant the bowsprit needed an extension called the **jibboom** or even a further extension known as the **flying jibboom** to carry the number of stays.

Ship identification by rigging (Diagram C)

Sloop	A Sloop has a single mast and two sails, a fore and aft rig (like a yacht today). The mast on a Sloop is closer to the bow of the boat than it would be on a Cutter, which has the same rig. The Sloop was fast and agile and needed few crew. It was mostly used in the coastal trade around Britain and Ireland.
Brig	A Brig had two masts only, a foremast and a mainmast. The foremast was square rigged, whilst the main mast had fore and aft sails and commonly two square rigged sails above them. It was the most common rig for smaller vessels under 200 tons and was used for both the coastal and short sea routes. It needed a larger crew than a sloop because of the square-rigged sails.
Brigantine	This was a two masted ship, smaller than a Brig, but with a similar rigging. The foremast was square-rigged, whilst the mainmast usually just had one big fore and aft sail, called the driver. However, it was not uncommon for one or two small square-rigged sails to be set above this. The less the number of square sails, the less crew required. It mostly served the coastal trade.
Barque	A Barque was a three masted ship; the fore and mainmasts were square- rigged and the mizzenmast was rigged fore and aft. With less work to do aloft, it was possible to have a smaller crew; this made it very attractive to merchants as it had speed and good cargo storage. As competition got stiffer in the second half of the 19th century (when steamships were beginning to have an impact) less crew became a very attractive proposition.
Schooner	Schooners had from two to four masts, all fore and aft rigged. The Schooners that sailed the coastal waters of the USA were most likely to be three to four masted, whereas the Schooners that sailed the UK coastal waters and into European waters were two to three masted vessels. Each of the fore and aft sails were supported by a gaff and fastened to a boom.
Ship	A fully rigged ship had three or four masts, all square rigged, with between three to five sails per mast. The mainmast was usually the tallest. It was commonplace for the full rigged ships to have up to four jib sails and sometimes a gaff sail on the mizzenmast.
Ketch	The ketch was the smallest two masted sailing vessel. The mainmast was considerably larger than the mizzenmast. Sometimes Ketches had very long bowsprits with several jib sails, to give it more speed and manoeuvrability. It was only ever used for coastal trading. Most fishing boats of this period had a very similar rig to a ketch.

Appendix 3
Early Lifeboats and their Inventors

What is a Lifeboat?

'Although the word lifeboat has not, in itself, any definite meaning, it is generally understood as signifying a boat specially constructed for saving life in storms and heavy seas when ordinary open boats could not attempt to do so except at the imminent peril or certain death to those within them….The principle causes of an open boat being unsafe in a heavy broken sea are, its liability to fill with water and swamp from a wave breaking into it or by upsetting, and loss of stability from all the water within it falling to one side, with every motion of the boat. It is therefore obvious that the chief requirement of a lifeboat is the counteraction as far as possible of these defects.'

Richard Lewis *History of the Lifeboat* (1874) p45

There is no absolute answer as to who 'invented' the first lifeboat; at least three competing claims exist.

Lionel Lukin and the UNIMMERGIBLE COBLE

Lionel Lukin, was born in Essex in 1742, and died in 1824. He was an inventor of many different artefacts, such as beds for the disabled, but is best known by the claim on his headstone, which he designed himself:

This Lionel Lukin was the first who built a lifeboat and was the original inventor of that principle of safety, by which many lives and much property have been preserved from shipwreck, and he obtained for it the King's patent in the year 1785.

In fact, the patent was awarded by the Prince of Wales (later George IV) for Lukin's 'unimmergible', which was a Norwegian yawl with watertight buoyancy chambers and a heavy false keel. It was not a commercially viable project and was never produced; however, he did transform a Northumberland coble (a flat-bottomed rowing boat) into a boat capable of saving lives at sea because it would not sink, even under the fiercest waves.

To Lionel Lukin, a coachbuilder of Long Acre, London, belongs the honour of inventing the lifeboat. As early as the year 1784 he designed and fitted a boat which was intended to save the lives of mariners wrecked on the coast. It had a projecting gunwale of cork and air-tight lockers or enclosures under the seats. These gave the boat great buoyancy, but it was liable to be disabled by having the sides stove in. Though Lukin was encouraged in his efforts by the Prince of Wales – afterwards George IV – his invention did not meet with the approval of those in power in the Admiralty and Lukin's only lifeboat which came into use was a coble that he fitted up for the Rev. Dr Sharp of Bamborough. For many years this was the only lifeboat on the coast and it is said to have saved many lives.

Extract from *Stories of the Lifeboat* **(1894) by Frank Mundell p11**

William Wouldhave and the Orange Segment Boat

William Wouldhave, born in 1751, died in 1821 was a parish clerk who turned his attention to the design of a boat that would save lives after a group of businessmen set up a prize for the best such invention; this followed the very public disaster that befell the collier ADVENTURE off the mouth of the Tyne in 1789. His design was innovative for the time… the boat was shaped like the segment of an orange, high at the bow and the stern and therefore difficult to capsize, but, while the Committee did not judge it to be the best of the designs submitted, they thought it interesting enough to offer him a prize of a guinea, which he rejected. His idea became the basic shape of the first viable lifeboat. Nonetheless, his headstone reads: *William Wouldhave, Inventor of that invaluable blessing to mankind… the Lifeboat.*

Henry Francis Greathead and the Curved Keel

Henry Francis Greathead, born in 1757, died in 1816, was the only one of the three Inventors to have a 'qualification' to design a lifeboat…he was a shipwright, working out of South Shields, on the Tyne. Although he entered the 1789 competition, his design also did not win but the Committee obviously saw him as the man to design a lifeboat that would be based on the ideas of other entrants. He called his lifeboat the ORIGINAL, as, although not all the ideas were his, it was the first practicable design for a working lifeboat. At 30 ft in length and 10 ft in width, it had a draught of only 3 ft, which made it ideal for working in the dangerous surf that so often claimed ships driven ashore. It seemed to combine the buoyancy/ballast ideas of Lukin, using cork extensively to pack the sides of the boat and under the seats, and the 'orange segment' shape of Wouldhave as the boat was higher in the bow and stern than in the middle. Greathead's addition was the heavy curved keel, that not only gave the boat its shallow draught but also helped its stability, making it much more difficult to remain capsized as it righted itself most of the time. It was, however, a cumbersome boat, having no rudder but just a large sweep oar; later models had two sweep oars to enable the boat to be steered either direction.

The honour of having been the first inventor of the lifeboat is also claimed by two other men, William Wouldhave and Henry Greathead. Both entered the competition set in 1789 by the Gentlemen of South Shields 'for the best model of a lifeboat calculated to brave the dangers of the sea, particularly in broken water.' After due consideration the prize was awarded to the shrewd boatbuilder at South Shields. He was instructed to build a boat on his own plan with several of Wouldhave's ideas introduced. This boat had 5 thwarts or seats for rowers, double banked to be manned by 10 oars; It was lined with cork and had a cork fender or pad outside, 16 inches deep. The chief point about Greathead's invention was that the keel was curved instead of being straight. This circumstance, simple as it appears, caused him to be regarded as the inventor of the first practicable lifeboat, for experience has proved that a boat with a curved keel is much more easily launched and beached than one with a straight keel… Lifeboats on this plan were afterwards placed on different parts of the coast and were the means of saving altogether some hundreds of lives.

Extracts from *Stories of the Lifeboat* (1894) by Frank Mundell p12–14

Many lifeboats were built to the specifications of the ORIGINAL, some lasting from 1790 to 1830; the oldest surviving lifeboat based on the design was the Zetland, which had 78 years of service.

Hundreds of lives were saved by the early lifeboats, but Frank Mundell tells of a sad disaster in 1810:

Though the lifeboats had done much good work, several disasters had befallen them, which caused many people to regard the remedy as worse than the disease. Of this there was a deplorable incident in 1810 when one of Greathead's lifeboats, manned by 15 men went to the rescue of some fishermen who had been caught in a gale off Tynemouth. They succeeded in taking the men onboard but on nearing the shore a huge wave swept the lifeboat on to a reef of rocks where she was smashed to atoms. 34 poor fellows – the rescued and the rescuers – were drowned. p15

Captain Marryat's LifeBoat

A letter from Captain Marryat to the Royal Humane Society in which he set out his design for a Life-Boat:

> The model of the boat I have the honour to present is 30 foot long, 8 foot wide and 3 foot deep…..the men are placed close to the side of the boat; by so doing they are removed as far as possible from the centre of motion…the oars are pulled upon an iron outrigger…. the bow and stern are both covered in two airtight partitions upon which no person can be placed so as to check her going through the waves; and the centre of the boat where men are to be stowed is so secure that it is impossible they be washed out unless the boat is upset. The interior construction of the boat is as follows: the centre is 19 feet long, 4 feet broad; at the bottom of this centre part of the boat is one solid foot of cork extending over the whole; this is pierced and grated over to allow free passage for any water she might ship. This cork is capable of supporting…more than the whole weight of men and iron-work in the boat; and as it spreads over a surface of 4 feet at the bottom of the boat, should the air-tight partition of one of the sides be stove in, it would sufficiently support the equilibrium of the boat, as to enable the men to use their oars and reach the shore. The rest of the boat is composed of six airtight divisions; the bow and stern are divided longitudinally which gives the advantage of increasing the number of partitions and also adds considerably to the strength of the boat. The side air partitions contain the seats of the rowers, who are fixed on them with leather aprons round their waist, that no water may enter …should she be swamped by a sea her specific lightness is such, that the water would immediately discharge itself through the holes at the bottom and she would rise without any assistance to her former draught of water…..the form of the lifeboat should be that of a whale boat…her bottom should be almost flat…her keel should be deep to give her a good grip in the water.
>
> The Gentlemen's Magazine of 1820 (Vol 90 Part 1 p444–445)

There is no record that Captain Marryat's boat was ever used in a rescue.

The Palmer Lifeboat

In the early days there was no central supervision or control of stations. George Palmer, an Essex MP, joined the Committee (Shipwreck Institution) in 1826 and two years later his plans for fitting lifeboats was adopted. Palmer's boats were in the form of a whale-boat, sharp at both ends but fuller at the bow (unlike Greathead's boats which could be rowed either way). There were three air cases on each side, one in the bows, two in the stern and these situated high up helped to prevent capsize and encouraged righting if the boat should be struck by a large sea.

Ray Kipling *Rescue by Sail and Oar* (1982) p6

In 1828, his plan of fitting lifeboats was used by the Institution and was only superseded in 1852 by the adoption of the self-righting principle. The services rendered by Palmer's boats to shipwrecked persons and vessels in distress were very great, some hundreds of the former having been saved through their instrumentality from inevitable death and many of the latter from destruction.

Richard Lewis *History of the Lifeboat* (1874) p16

The Plenty Lifeboat

William Plenty moved from Southampton to Newbury in 1790 and set up business as a maker of agricultural equipment. He designed his first lifeboat around 1815/1816. When the Royal National Institution for Preserving Lives from shipwreck was founded in 1824, 11 out of the 14 lifeboats stationed around the country were built by Mr Plenty of Newbury. Both his sons, James and Edward Pellew, joined the family firm and in 1851 were placed third with their entry into the competition set up by the Duke of Northumberland; it was an improved model of their father's original lifeboat. Their model was displayed at the Great Exhibition in 1851; however, the design was overtaken by the Peake self-righting boat and the firm stopped producing Plenty lifeboats by the end of the 1860's.

Another standard design was that of Pellew Plenty of Newbury. His boats at 24 feet, almost 3 feet shorter than Palmer's….extra buoyancy came from air-cases but there was no ballast and no provision for self-righting. There were six scuppers for freeing the boats of water and although the internal shape of the boat was designed to make shipped water roll out again, this was not very effective.

Ray Kipling *Rescue by Sail and Oar* (1982) p78

The Liverpools

Another class of boats were named the Liverpools. They had 12 oars, 2 sprit sails and a jib, and were 30 feet long. Initially they had no means of freeing themselves of water, but relieving tubes were added in 1850.

Ray Kipling *Rescue by Sail and Oar* (1982) p8

However, according to Ray Kipling:

In the RNLI's view lifeboats have nothing to do with sails and they should be forbidden in most, if not all cases... In 1857 the RNLI Committee of Management issued the instruction "Coxswains are to be informed that they are never to use their sails, unless the distance to the scene of the wreck is too great to be reached by rowing and that, as a general rule, when running for land before a heavy sea, they will invariably, if practicable, take in their sails before going into the broken water. p13

Appendix 4
The Peake SR (self-righting) Lifeboat

What made the Peake SR superior to any existing boat design of the time was the combination of features which meant it addressed most, if not all, of the concerns about the Palmer and Plenty boats.

The following extracts are all taken from Richard Lewis *History of the Lifeboat* (1874).

Self-Righting

The real difference between an ordinary and a Self-Righting boat is that while the former on being thrown by the sea or other force on one side, beyond a certain angle offers no further resistance and cannot return, the latter on the contrary continues to oppose such a force in every position in which it can be placed… The Self-Righting power is obtained by the following means: 1st: The boat is built with a considerable sheer of gunwale, the bow and stern being from 1 foot 6 inches to 2 feet higher than the sides of the boat at her centre; and the space within the boat at either extremity…is enclosed by a sectional bulkhead and a ceiling and so converted into a water-tight air-chamber… 2ndly: A heavy iron keel is attached and a nearly equal weight of light air cases and cork ballast cases is stowed betwixt the boat's floor and the deck… when the boat is forcibly placed in the water with keel upwards, she is floated unsteadily on the two air-chambers at bow and stern, whilst the heavy iron keel and other ballast being then carried above the centre of gravity, an unstable equilibrium is at once effected; the raised weight falls one side or the other of the centre of gravity and drags the boat round to her ordinary position, when the water shipped during the evolution quickly escapes. p56–57

Self-Ejecting or Self-Discharging

The second peculiar characteristic of a lifeboat… is the capability of self-discharging in a few seconds any water which may be shipped by the breaking over of a sea, or by a boat being suddenly thrown on her beam ends… This self-discharging power is accomplished by means of the water-tight deck at the load water-line and a sufficient number of large open tubes, having their upper orifices at the surface of the deck and their lower ones at the boat's floor, passing through the space between the deck and the floor but hermetically

Diagram D:
Specifications
of a Peake SR.

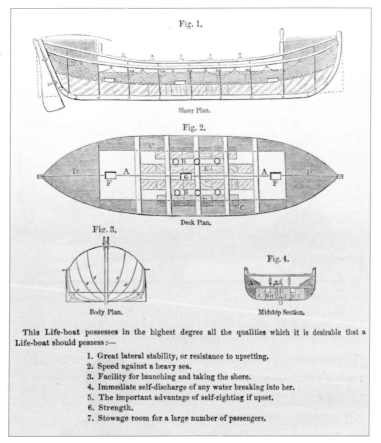

Fig. 1.

Sheer Plan.

Fig. 2.

Deck Plan.

Fig. 3.

Body Plan.

Fig. 4.

Midship Section.

This Life-boat possesses in the highest degree all the qualities which it is desirable that a Life-boat should possess:—

1. Great lateral stability, or resistance to upsetting.
2. Speed against a heavy sea.
3. Facility for launching and taking the shore.
4. Immediate self-discharge of any water breaking into her.
5. The important advantage of self-righting if upset.
6. Strength.
7. Stowage room for a large number of passengers.

closed to it; thus providing an open communication between the interior of the boat and the sea, yet without suffering any leakage into the air-chambers under the deck… In the Self-Righting boats the tubes are fitted with self-acting valves which open downwards only, so that they will not allow any water shipped to pass downwards whilst none beyond a trifling leakage can pass upwards through them. p48–49

Ballasting

We may here observe that ballast of some kind is very contributive to the efficiency of a lifeboat. Not only must it add to her stability and therefore her safety, but in proportion to the heaviness of the sea does weight become necessary to insure speed, its momentum being requisite to withstand the blow of each succeeding breaker and carry the boat through as it strikes her…The Institutions Self-Righting lifeboats are first ballasted with an iron keel, which acts as a most powerful leverage. Ballast formed of air-tight cases and of cork enclosed in water-tight cases is also used in the self-righting boats of the Institution of nearly equal weight to the iron keel. p51–52

Description of a Peake SR Lifeboat

The Peake adaptation of Beeching's model became the RNLI standard Self-Righting pulling and sailing lifeboat, which was constantly adapted and improved. The disadvantage of normal open boats in rough seas are that they cannot clear water if they are swamped, they will not right if they are capsized and any water in the boat will roll from side to side, like a shifting cargo affecting stability. The Peake lifeboat therefore had extra buoyancy, self-discharging of water, ballasting, self-righting, stability, speed, storage room and inherent strength. The buoyancy was provided by water-tight air-cases fitted inside the boat and by high end cases at the bow and stern which also helped with self-righting. The self-discharge of water was helped by a number of open tubes being let into the watertight deck. The tubes had a valve which opened downwards only to allow water to drain out. Ballast was need to add stability and to give the boat sufficient momentum to drive through breakers… Self-Righting boats had a heavy iron keel… air-cases and cork in water-tight cases added to the ballast, the cork's weight giving stability and its density giving buoyancy if the boat was damaged… Stability came from the iron keel, for although a broader beam would have given more stability, it would also have reduced speed… the boat had to be heavy enough to push through waves without losing all her way and strong enough to withstand crashing down into the trough.

Ray Kipling *Rescue By Sail and Oar* (1982) p14

Appendix 5
RNLI Boat Houses & their Equipment

The Boat House

Fortunately, the Institution was enabled in 1857 to secure the services of Mr CH Cooke FRIBA as its Hon Architect and his co-operation in connection with the erection of Lifeboat Houses has been invaluable. From his plans and specifications upwards of 200 Houses have been constructed at different Lifeboat Stations. Thus, substantial and well-built Houses have been provided. In respect to those sites, regard is particularly taken to their convenience so that they may be handy for launching the lifeboat and for her easy transport on her carriage along the coast to the scene of a wreck. The House is usually 40 feet long and 17 feet wide – its doors are 14 feet wide and their height about 12 feet. There are folding doors of the above dimensions facing the water and if it should be deemed an advantage to be able to take the boat on her carriage to the rear of the House, doors of the same dimension are also placed at that end. The Lifeboat House is usually a substantial building, built of brick and stone and having a slated roof.

Richard Lewis *History of the Lifeboat* (1874) p110–112

(47) Boat House at Bude, Cornwall 1880's

The basic design and dimensions of Cooke's plans were applied to all Boat Houses built in this period. However, builders around the country added their own interpretations to the mandatory design, with the result that the remaining examples of Boat Houses show some individuality, as well as the well-known outline of an RNLI Boat House.

(48) Tyrella Lifeboat House (2018). View of front door

(49) Tyrella Lifeboat House (2018). View of rear door

Inside the Boat House

"A boarding or flooring about 6 feet in length is placed over the joists at the rear of the House to keep the spare stores on; and a batten with wooden pegs for hanging up the lifebelts and small lines to be fixed at a convenient height along the side wall."

Richard Lewis *History of the Lifeboat* (1874) p112

Obviously, if the lifeboat had to have access to both rear and front doors, there would not be flooring obstructing the rear door. In these cases, the stores were placed elsewhere, often the rafters.

The photos above show the Tyrella Boat House. While the front entrance has been altered, the rear opening is the original and would have been the exit route for the lifeboat when being horsed to a rescue.

Around the walls of the lifeboat house, there would have been poster-size notices such as RULES FOR THE TREATMENT OF THE APPARENTLY DROWNED and RNLI LIFEBOAT REGULATIONS.

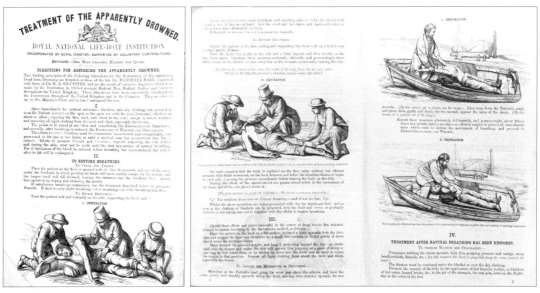

(50) Rules for the Treatment of the Apparently Drowned

Some stations may have had Service Boards, commemorating the shouts of previous lifeboats, and/or a list of the contributors to the Branch. Later in the 19th century and early 20th century boathouses were equipped with telegraphic communication, which made getting information about ships in distress much quicker.

Life-belts

A most welcome innovation was the life-belt which had become mandatory apparel for any lifeboatman going afloat by 1854. The earliest published description of a life preserver was almost a century before, when, in 1759, Dr J Wilkinson unveiled his idea of a jacket made of thin sailcloth, without sleeves and lined with 3/4" thick cork, each piece being 6" broad & 16" in length. They were sewed in sections like pockets. The jacket resembled a waistcoat, fastened with cork buttons. There is no record of it ever being made. Various other "Life-Preservers' were mentioned in newspaper and journal articles in the late 18th and early 19th centuries; there is no indication that any of the inventions were ever commercially used.

The variations in possible life-savers had been trialled, under the supervision of Commander J R Ward, and whilst the air-filled bags gave the best buoyancy, they were too liable to puncture. The adopted design was a vest, which had narrow strips of cork sewn into canvas pockets and secured front and back by strings, later replaced with more substantial canvas material and

(51) Lifeboat crew wearing oil skins, boots & sou'westers c1890.

buckles. It was fastened at the waist, so that there was no extra pressure on the chest, enabling the wearer to breathe normally. Being tied in the middle, it could not float off whilst on the wearer, or, even worse, turn him over in the water.

This would then make it virtually impossible for the wearer to right himself again. As we have seen, this was the tragic fate in 1868 of Robert Boyd, the Ballywalter coxswain, who had neglected to tie his life-belt correctly before going afloat.

It was a bulky waistcoat on top of the lifeboatmen's ordinary clothes but was sufficiently buoyant to support a fully clothed man; additionally the insulation of the cork helped to prevent heat loss from the body when immersed in water. It was initially viewed with some scepticism by lifeboat crews, who, as fishermen, had sailed all their lives at sea without such an item. However, after the Whitby disaster of 1861, when it was noted that the only lifeboatman saved, Henry Freeman, had also been the only crew member wearing a life-belt, other crews accepted more readily the 'imposition' of wearing the bulky vest.

The lifebelts were stored in the Boat House after each 'shout', drying out on their pegs. It was the responsibility of the coxswain to ensure their care and maintenance, and he would have examined them now and again, as they hung from their pegs, for wear and tear. Any problems and the coxswain would have reported the matter to the Secretary , who would then have informed the District Inspector. After an inspection he would have ordered any necessary repairs or replacement. In this way, equipment was kept under constant scrutiny.

Crew Clothing

In the early years of the Lifeboats, there would have been no personal equipment provided, other than the Life-belts. This was because lifeboat crews were virtually all volunteer fishermen and Coastguards who would certainly have had their own clothing suitable for going to sea in all weathers. This would have included guernseys or ganseys/jerseys/arans (all named after the respective Islands) which were garments knitted from oiled wool, rich in lanolin.

Rarely washed, these made the jumpers very windproof but relatively light and easy to move around in. In wet weather, the men would wear oilskins, initially coarse linen garments, soaked in linseed oil and left to cure for a long time. The end result was a windproof and waterproof coat, ideal for the lifeboat. Most would also have worn sou'westers (said to take its name from the south-westerlies… winds which were known to bring the rain). These were oilskin hats that

(52) Lifeboatman wearing sou'wester and cork life-jacket over his "Gansey".

were longer at the back than the front, in order to give the neck coverage from rain running down inside the collar of the oilskin; these hats often had a 'gutter brim' which prevented the rain from streaming down the wearer's face and potentially obstructing their view. By the end of the century some stations had 'spare' oilskins and sou'westers for the crew who were no longer fishermen, but farm labourers or other locals. Most of the men would also have worn thigh high waders or boots, which would have been found in most sea-side households of the time.

Equipment for the Boat

Sails

Some Lifeboats were equipped with sails, made of canvas, with different kinds of rigging depending on the type of coastline / tidal estuaries that the lifeboat was working. The amount of sail carried was small, as lifeboats were designed for rough weather, so only storm sails were sensible. Much skill was needed to handle the sailing lifeboats, judging how far out to row before setting the sails when launching or when to take the sails in when returning to shore. Sudden shifts in wind could catch out the inexperienced and cause disaster.

Small Lines

Hanging on the wooden pegs in the Boat House were small lines, or ropes. These could have included a spare throwing line, with a small grapnel attached at the end, used to secure the lifeboat to any ship it had come alongside, in order to make getting the crew off the ship easier. There could also have been spare lines for throwing to people already in the water so that they could be pulled in towards the lifeboat and then helped on board. Finally there may have been replacement life-lines which were:

> …attached round the entire length of the boat, to which persons in the water may cling till they can be got into the boat; the two central lines are festooned lower than the others to be used as a stirrups, so that a person in the water, by stepping on them, may climb into the boat without assistance.

Richard Lewis *History of the Lifeboat* (1874) p72

The Drogue

The drogue was:

> …a conical canvas bag about 4 feet long, one end being two feet in diameter, the other end

4 inches in diameter. The drogue was towed astern when beaching the boat or running before a heavy breaking sea. It acted as a brake or sea anchor and by keeping the boat stern to the sea, prevented her being swept broadside to the waves or broaching. The drogue could be worked to deal with each wave; a tripping line brought the narrow end around and reduced the braking effect.

Ray Kipling *Rescue By Sail and Oar* (1982) p25

RNLI Minutes (October 24 1871) had noted that the drogue at the Tyrella station did not appear to be reliable for a heavy drag and so it was replaced. The Coxswain would have noted any defects or wear and tear in equipment, reported it to the Hon Secretary, who in turn would have informed the RNLI. An Inspector would then have checked on the condition of the item(s) and ordered replacements or repair if necessary.

Oars

One of the most important pieces of equipment for a lifeboat were the oars. Indeed, so important were they that every lifeboat had to carry spare oars strapped under the thwarts whilst afloat on service, in case of breakages (against rocks, wreckage, ships or even just in heavy seas).

Oars breaking on rescue worried the RNLI, so a series of trials were carried out in 1866, looking at the qualities of lightness, stiffness and strength in 38 oars of various woods and weights…..oars fashioned from whole young trees in the Norway and Baltic woods proved best.

Ray Kipling *Rescue By Sail and Oar* (1982) p27

Oars were painted white or blue, depending on whether they were used on the port side of the boat (white oars) or starboard side of the boat (blue oars). This was to allow the cox to shout instructions to the lifeboatmen that could be heard over howling winds and crashing waves. The terms in use at the time 'starboard' and 'larboard' were too easily confused in bad weather; the Cox would shout 'white' and the rowers on the port side of the boat would pull, whilst the blue oars men raised their oars slightly, parallel to the water (known as feathering) and the boat would turn to the starboard; the obverse instructions were called if the cox wanted to turn the boat to port. The oars were attached to the boat initially with a rope grommet so that they could lie alongside the boat, instead of shipping them when alongside a ship. Even when the swivel

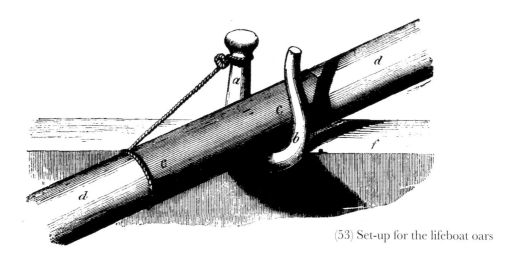

(53) Set-up for the lifeboat oars

crutch was developed, the oar was still attached to a rope lanyard, so it could be retained when hanging over the side.

> The biggest effort on the oars was needed usually at the launch. The coxswain would shout the order to slip, and on the order… rowing started… The first two pulls had to be strong enough to carry the boat into the oncoming wave; the third would be almost lost in the foam. Curiously, it was common to have 13 men in a crew: a coxswain, second coxswain, bowman and ten oarsmen. There seemed to be no superstition about this…
>
> **Ray Kipling *Rescue By Sail & Oar* (1982) p27**

Transporting Carriage

The design of the carriage was often referred to as 'ingenious'. It was designed so that the boat's weight rested on the large wheel but rollers assisted in the sliding of the boat off its keelway when the horses were detached and the keelway lowered into the water; the reverse process worked for getting the boat back onto the carriage before the horses were harnessed to pull her back into shore.

> The boat is hauled off the carriage and launched into the sea by a rope at each end of the boat rove through the sheeve D, having one end hooked to a self-detaching hook at the boat's stern and the other manned by a few persons on the shore, who thus hauled the

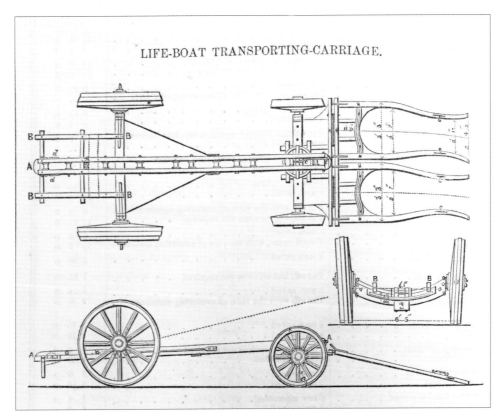

LIFE-BOAT TRANSPORTING-CARRIAGE.

Diagram E: Life-Boat transporting carriage.

boat and her crew off the carriage and launched them afloat at once, with their oars in their hands, by which means headway may be obtained before the breakers have time to beat the boat back broadside on to the beach."

The Lifeboat 1 April 1861 p398

The carriage was used not only for normal launches from the Boat House, but also to transport the lifeboat to the closest point to the reported ship in distress. This was much more time saving than the lifeboatmen having to row (or sail) the distance before they could even begin their rescue. Horses were used to haul the lifeboat onto the beach or across by road to the site of the distressed ship. It had become an offense, punishable by a fine of £100, not to supply horses for a lifeboat in need, unless there was a reasonable excuse.

Appendix 6
Table showing seasonal occurrence of wrecks at Tyrella 1747–1897

Based on statistics for ships wrecked and grounded from St John's Point to Dundrum Bay

Time of Year	Number of Wrecks	% of wrecks
January to December	220	100
No month given for wreck	2	1
Winter: November–February	124	58
Spring: March–May	36	16
Summer: June–August	23	10
Autumn: September–October	34	15
Worst Month January	54	25

Map 6: Irish lifeboat stations
c1830–1900

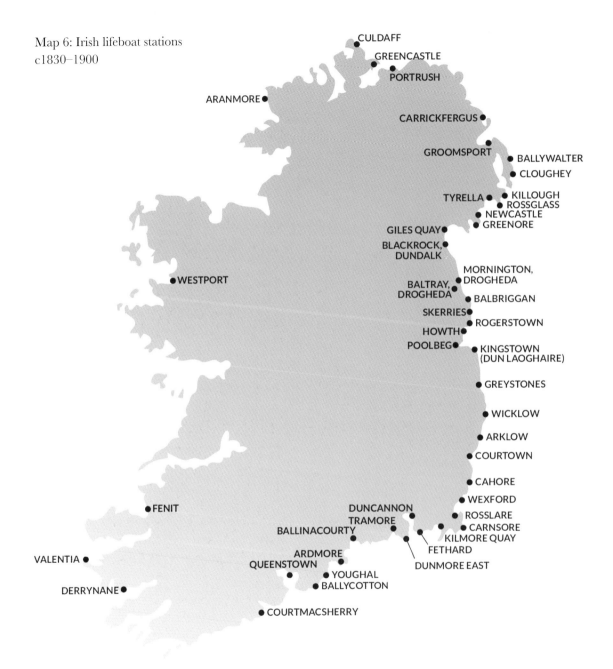

Appendix 7
Table to show launches and lives saved
Irish Lifeboat Stations of the 19th and early 20th centuries

Based on statistics provided in Nicholas Leach *Lifeboat Stations of Ireland* p117–255

Station	Years	Launches	Lives saved
Rosslare/Rosslare Fort	1858–1900	92	174
Arklow	1826–30; 1857–1913	96	174
Wexford No 2	1866–1897	45	170
Ballywalter	1866–1906	37	154
Courtown	1865–1903	46	150
Ballinacourty (Dungarven)	1859–1900	39	137
Carnsore	1859–1897	34	130
Tyrella	1838–51; 1860–1899	37	103
Tramore	1858–1898	27	101
Wicklow	1857–1911	54	99
Howth	1817–43; 1860–1899	33	96
Ballycotton	1858–1930	34	88
Newcastle	1830–33; 1854–1906	37	86
Black Rock, Dundalk	1859–1909	33	75
Portrush	1860–1902	24	71
Groomsport	1858–1901	29	67
Cahore	1857–1916	57	66
Baltray, Drogheda	1856–1899	30	59
Skerries	1833–1903	18	57
Cloughey	1885–1906	32	54
Kingstown (Dun Laoghaire) No 1	1817–1899	26	53

Station	Years	Launches	Lives saved
Duncannon	1869–1886	8	43
Youghal	1839–1906	24	41
Mornington, Drogheda	1883–1902	28	38
Poolbeg	1815–1900	28	34
Fenit	1879–1895	18	30
Aranmore	1888–1902	17	29
Courtmacsherry	1825–1901	21	24
Greencastle	1864–1902	24	24
Dun Laoghaire No 2	1890–1913	21	24
Rossglass/St John's Point	1825–1843	4	20
Giles Quay, Dundalk	1880–1912	12	19
Dunmore East	To 1911	11	16
Rosslare Harbour	1896–1911	18	14
Queenstown (Crosshaven)	1866–1920	22	13
Carrick	1896–1913	11	10
Ardmore	1858–1895	3	7
Greystones	1872–1896	3	4
Valentia	1864–1896	10	0
Greenore	1894–1920	10	0
Kilmore Quay	1848–1901	9	0
Fethard	1886–1898	5	0
Killough	1901–1914	3	0
Culduff	1892–1913	2	0
Balbriggan	1875–1898	2	0
Westport	1857–1862	0	0
Rogerstown	1874–1882	0	0
Derrynane	1844–1855	0	0

Appendix 8

The following tables are the Service Records for the Tyrella Lifeboats 1838–1899

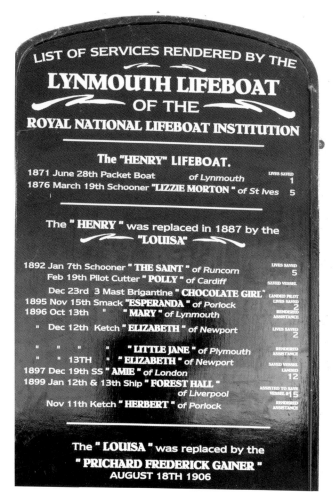

(54) This is the service board for Lynmouth 1899, there are no service boards surviving for Tyrella.

1st Tyrella Lifeboat 1838–1852

Date	Ship	Service	Lives saved	Awards made	Location of service	Weather conditions	Source of information
29.11.1838	*British Heroine*	Rescued whole crew in three trips	20	RNLI gave cash award; Lloyd's gave £20.00	Tyrella	'Fierce gale'	RNLI Case 674; *Newry Telegraph*
28.01.1840	*Trevor*	Saved crew	?	–	Driven ashore close to Tyrella Coastguard Station	'South-East gale'	*Shipping & Mercantile Gazette*
17.01.1845	*Frolic*	Lifeboat swamped; but Taylor (CG) rescued crew with local fishermen	6	RNIPLS Silver Medal to James Taylor	Driven ashore at Tyrella	'South-East gale'	*Downpatrick Recorder*
17.12.1847	*Ida*	Lifeboat failed to save crew	0	RNIPLS cash award to crew	Ballyvaston, Tyrella	'Great storm raging'	*Newry Telegraph*; Letter in RNLI Archives
17.12.1847	*Lowther*	Lifeboat rescued crew	?	RNIPLS cash award to crew	Ballyvaston, Tyrella	'Great storm raging'	*Newry Telegraph*; Letter in RNLI Archives
06.04.1850	*Sarah Ann*	Lifeboat saved crew	?	–	'In great distress off Tyrella'	No mention	*Downpatrick Recorder*

1st RNLI Lifeboat '*The Tyrella*' (1860–1866)

Date	Ship	Service	Lives saved	Awards made	Location of service	Weather conditions	Source of information
17.10.1860	*Martha Whitmore*	Lifeboat horsed 6 miles but not required	–	–	St John's Point	'South-Westerly gale'	*Belfast Morning News*
12.06.1861	*John Bull*	Lifeboat horsed and launched but not required	–	–	Between St John's Point & Ballyvaston	'Dense fog and south-east gale'	*Downpatrick Recorder*; *Belfast Daily Mercury*
27.09.1861	*Glasgow*	Crew rescued by lifeboat	?	–	Driven ashore in Dundrum Bay	Not mentioned	Lloyd's Lists
11.01.1862	*Solferino*	Lifeboat launched; out all night but not needed	–	–	Rathmullen	'Heavy seas'	RNLI Archives
17.01.1862	*Bellona*	Rescued only surviving crew from rigging	1	–	Dundrum Bar	'Heavy seas and fierce gale'	*Belfast Morning News*
02.01.1864	*Hamilton Gray*	Newcastle Lifeboat damaged in rescue; Tyrella boat assisted	–	–	Southern end of Dundrum Bay	'Heavy gale of wind'	Lloyd's Lists; *Oxford Times*
18.11.1864	*Rook* and *Cottager*	Tyrella lifeboat went out to assist both; crew able to get off	–	–	Between Minerstown and Rossglass	'Dangerously high seas'	*Waterford Mail*
06.12.1865	*Daniel O'Connell*	Horsed close to site; rescued all crew	5	–	Rathmullen	'very heavy surf'	*Belfast News Letter*; *Illustrated Times*

2nd RNLI Lifeboat: 'The Tyrella' (ii) 1866–1875

Date	Ship	Service	Lives saved	Awards made	Location of service	Weather conditions	Source of information
24.03.1867	William of Paimpol	Lifeboat took 3 goes to get to ship for rescue	6	-	1 mile from Tyrella Coastguard Station	'gale and heavy seas'	Western Daily Press
19.04.1867	Charlotte Harrison	Lifeboat went out to ship; remained all night. Not needed.	-	-	Anchored between Cow & Calf and Coastguard Station	'thick fog and gale from south'	Cardiff Times
06.02.1870	Eliza	Lifeboat launched but help not needed	-	-	Dundrum Bay	Heavy gale	RNLI Archives
02.01.1871	Colima	Lifeboat went out twice to rescue crew	?	-	Onshore near Dundrum bar	'Gale unparalleled in intensity for 20 years'	Downpatrick Recorder; Glasgow Herald
04.03.1871	William	Lifeboat went out; crew saved; accounts differ who saved them	5?	-	Grounded at Minerstown	'Fierce southerly'	Newry Telegraph; Belfast Morning News
09.03.1871	Isabella	Lifeboat went out; crew able to get off	-	-	Stranded 'soft sands at Tyrella'	South Easterly gale	Downpatrick Recorder
16.08.1872	Neptunus	Lifeboat got through heavy surf to rescue whole crew	14	'Thanks on Vellum' to John Williams	Stranded close to Tyrella Coastguard Station	'south-south easterly gale'	Cardiff Times; Downpatrick Recorder

Date	Ship	Service	Lives saved	Awards made	Location of service	Weather conditions	Source of information
28.11.1874	*Donna Maria*	Lifeboat horsed & launched; got crew off; had to go back for trapped seaman	6	Silver medals to Adam Murphy, John Gordon & 'Thanks on Vellum' to James Foland	Ballyvaston	'Violent gale from sea; bitter and incessant rain'	*Downpatrick Recorder*; Lloyd's Lists.
30.11.1874	*Unknown*	Lifeboat went out and rescued crew	3	–	Capsized in Dundrum Bay	'Heavy gale from the south-east'	*Sheffield Daily Telegraph*
26.02.1875	*Friends*	Lifeboat rescued crew	4	–	Anchored in Dundrum Bay, trying to round St John's Point	'Easterly gale; sea was much broken'	*Belfast Newsletter*; *The Lifeboat* (RNLI Journal)
19.10.1875	*Lizzie*	Lifeboat launched; rescued crew	?	–	Dundrum Bay	No mention	Lloyd's Lists

3rd RNLI Lifeboat: 'The Memorial' (1876–1888)

Date	Ship	Service	Lives saved	Awards made	Location of service	Weather Conditions	Source of information
02.01.1876	Ellen	Lifeboat horsed to site and launched; not needed	–	–	Driven ashore near Black Rock, Rathmullen	'Strong south-easterly gale'	RNLI Archives
15.11.1876	Aulini Sinai	Lifeboat horsed and launched, crew were saved	6	–	'Dolly Rocks' Minerstown	'gale from the south and a very rough sea'	Belfast Weekly News; Manchester Times
09.04.1877	Ocean Packet no 3	Lifeboat found ship abandoned	–	–	Dundrum Bay	'South east gale'	RNLI Archives
13.04.1878	Cygnet	Lifeboat saved crew	4	–	Driven ashore close to Coastguard Station	'Very heavy seas'	Lloyd's Lists; Morning Post
22.09.1878	Wasp	Lifeboat rescued crew	3	–	Stranded near Tyrella	No mention	Freeman's Journal
05.11.1880	Olaf Kyrie	Lifeboat stayed alongside until ship rounded St John's Pt	–	–	St John's Point	Severe south-easterly changed to westerly	RNLI Archives
07.02.1881	Bransty	Great difficulty getting off beach because of breakers	4	–	Long Rocks, Tyrella	'severe gale from the south east & a very heavy sea'	Downpatrick Recorder; Manchester Times
29.09.1881	Gertrude	Lifeboat took off crew that wanted to leave	13	–	Stranded on rocks, Minerstown	No mention	Belfast News Letter

Date	Ship	Service	Lives saved	Awards made	Location of service	Weather Conditions	Source of information
14.08.1883	*Henry*	Lifeboat horsed to Pt; stayed alongside all night; assisted in anchoring	5	–	St John's Point	'strong south-east gale, and rain'	*Belfast Evening Telegraph*; *St James' Gazette*
09.02.1884	*Victoria*	Lifeboat horsed and launched; survivors not found	0	–	Rathmullen	'Heavy gale and bitter rain'	*Newry Telegraph*; *Downpatrick Recorder*
21.01.1885	*Mary Hellen*	Lifeboat launched but not needed; crew got to shore	–	–	Dundrum Bay	'south east gale'	RNLI Archives
21.02.1885	*Helen*	Lifeboat rescued crew	4	–	Sands at Tyrella Coastguard Station	'dreadful gale'	*The Scotsman*
08.08.1885	*Rambler*	Daring rescue because of hidden rocks	4	–	Ringsallen Point, Tyrella	'full force of a south-easterly gale'	*Dublin Daily Express*; *Gloucester Citizen*
27.02.1886	*Barclay*	Took 2 goes to get off beach; dangerous hidden reefs; all rescued	5 crew and 2 children	RNLI checked but no award	Smith's Rock, Tyrella	'furious south-east gale and snowstorm raging'	*Belfast News Letter*; *Hull Daily Mail*
24.01.1887	*Esperance*	Lifeboat rescued crew	10	–	Sank in Dundrum Bay	'thick weather'	*Sunderland Daily Echo*

4th RNLI Lifeboat: '*Louisa Burnaby*' (1888–1899)

Date	Ship	Service	Lives saved	Awards	Location of services	Weather conditions	Source of information
13.11.1888	*Wild Rose*	Lifeboat rescued part of crew and landed them at Dundrum	5	–	Off Dundrum	No mention	*Manchester Times*
19.08.1889	*Fly*	Lifeboat went out; secured Pilot; owner refused to pay RNLI crew fees. Court case to recover.	–	–	Dundrum Bar	'wind was blowing south, right on the shore'	*Belfast News Letter; Lancashire Evening Post*
14.01.1894	*Mary Ann*	Went out to assist ship as she anchored but not needed.	–	–	Close to shore at Rathmullen	'south-easterly gale'	*London Evening Standard*
14.01.1894	*Lady Arthur Hill*	Steamship had difficulty crossing Bar but lifeboat not eventually needed	–	–	Dundrum Bar	'south-easterly gale'	*Downpatrick Recorder*
12.07.1895	Fishing boat	Went out to brothers whose boat capsized;	2	–	Cow & Calf Rocks, Tyrella	'caught in a squall'	*Northern Whig*
24.12.1895	Full rigged ship	Went out to assist ship to anchor till wind changed to SW	–	–	St John's Point	''south-easterly gale and heavy sea'	*Cardiff Times*

Footnotes

Introduction: The Forgotten Lifeboats of Tyrella
i. www: portaferrylifeboat.com (section on The Ballywalter Lifeboat)
ii. *Irish News* 5 November 1965
iii. *Down Recorder* 29 April 1992

Chapter 1: A Dangerous Bay
i. John Hanna 'Gossipings About…' *Downpatrick Recorder* 13 October 1860
ii. Walter Harris '*Ancient and Present State of the County Down*' (1744) p120
iii. *Sailing Ships of Mourne* (1971) p95
iv. Ian Cameron *Riders of the Storm* (2002) p13
v. ibid p19
vi. Nicholas Leach *The Lifeboat Service in Ireland* (2005) p25
vii. PRONI Downshire Papers D671/C/147/38
viii. PRONI Downshire Papers D671/C/147/40
ix. *Newry Telegraph* 26 October 1837
x. *Dublin Evening Packet* 20 September 1837
xi. *Downpatrick Recorder* 27 January 1838
xii. *Downpatrick Recorder* 26 February 1842

Chapter 2: Enter the Lifeboat
i. *Downpatrick Recorder* 26 May 1855
ii. Nautical Magazine & Naval Chronicles for 1867 p42
iii. *Weekly Vindicator* 5 May 1849
iv. Ian Cameron *Riders of the Storm* (2002) p39
v. Oliver Warner *The Lifeboat Service* (1974) p22
vi. Ian Cameron *Riders of the Storm* (2002) p46
vii. ibid p33
viii. Oliver Warner *The Lifeboat Service* (1974) p41
ix. *Northern Whig* 14 March 1840
x. *Vindicator* 11 April 1840

xi. Parliamentary Inquiry into Tidal Harbours 4 October 1845
xii. *Thom's Irish Almanac and Official Directory* (1851) p539
xiii. Nicholas Leach *Lifeboats in Ireland* p20
xiv. ibid p20
xv. ibid p21
xvi. Oliver Warner *The Lifeboat Service* p24
xvii. Committee Minutes of the National Lifeboat Institution 15 November 1838
xviii. Case 674 (RNLI Archives)
xix. *Newry Telegraph* 29 November 1838
xx. ibid 29 March 1839
xxi. *Downpatrick Recorder* 2 February 1845
xxii. *Newry Telegraph* 21 December 1847
xxiii. Case 998 (RNLI Archives)
xxiv. *Downpatrick Recorder* 6 April 1850
xxv. *Belfast News Letter* 9 December 1859

Chapter 3: Re-birth
i. Richard Lewis *The History of the Lifeboat* p20–21
ii. Ian Cameron *Riders of the Storm* p51
iii. ibid p53
iv. *Southern Reporter & Cork Commercial Courier* 29 November 1861
v. Richard Lewis *The History of the Lifeboat* p2
vi. *Downpatrick Recorder* 28 January 1860

Chapter 4: *The Tyrella*
i. RNLI Inspectors' Reports Book C p105
ii. *Belfast Morning News* 30 January 1860
iii. *Manchester Courier & Lancashire General Advertiser* 7 April 1860
iv. *Freeman's Journal* 22 September 1860
v. *Downshire Protestant* 8 October 1860
vi. *Downpatrick Recorder* 6 October 1860
vii. Oliver Warner *History of the Lifeboat* (1974) p45

viii. *Downpatrick Recorder* 6 October 1860

ix. *Belfast Morning News* 22 October 1860

x. Richard Lewis *A History of the Lifeboat* (1874) p79

xi. *Downpatrick Recorder* 2 February 1861

xii. *Downpatrick Recorder* 15 June 1861

xiii. *Belfast Daily Mercury* 17 July 1861

xiv. *Belfast News Letter* 27 July 1861

xv. Dibdin & Ayling *The Book of the Lifeboat* (1894) p26

xvi. *Belfast Morning News* 17 January 1862

xvii. *Downpatrick Recorder* 8 February 1862

xviii. RNLI Annual Report May 15 1875 p234

xix. *Belfast News Letter* 12 December 1865

xx. Richard Lewis *A History of the Lifeboat* (1874) p139

xxi. RNLI Inspectors' Reports Book C p105–106

Chapter 5: Change and Controversy

i. *Downpatrick Recorder* 22 December 1866

ii. *Western Daily Press* 20 March 1869

iii. Richard Lewis *A History of the Lifeboat* (1874) p113–114

iv. *Belfast Weekly News* 2 June 1869

v. Richard Lewis *A History of the Lifeboat* (1874) p104–105

vi. *Cardiff Times* 27 April 1867

vii. RNLI Inspector's Report Book C p107

viii. *Downpatrick Recorder* 21 January 1871

ix. *Downpatrick Recorder* 18 March 1871

x. RNLI Inspector's Report Book C p107–108

xi. ibid

xii. as quoted in *Downpatrick Recorder* 1 August 1874

xiii. *Downpatrick Recorder* 9 November 1872

xiv. RNLI Inspector's Report Book F p407

xv. *Downpatrick Recorder* 5 December 1874

xvi. *Downpatrick Recorder* 12 December 1874

xvii. *Downpatrick Recorder* 19 December 1874

xviii. *Downpatrick Recorder* 19 December 1874

xix. *Downpatrick Recorder* 6 January 1869

xx. *Downpatrick Recorder* 8 July 1872

xxi. *Belfast Weekly News* 8 June 1878

xxii. *Daily Telegraph* 8 January 1875

xxiii. as reported in *Belfast News Letter* 2 August 1875

Chapter 6: The Memorial

i. RNLI Inspector's Report Book C p108

ii. RNLI Inspector's Report Book F p 407–408

iii. *Downpatrick Recorder* 1 January 1876

iv. RNLI Inspector's Report Book F p409

v. *Belfast Weekly News* 18 November 1876

vi. *Belfast News Letter* 11 October 1881

vii. *Belfast Evening Telegraph* 16 August 1883

viii. Richard Lewis *A History of the Lifeboat* (1874) p79

ix. *Dublin Daily Express* 12 August 1885

x. *Gloucester Citizen* 12 August 1885

xi. *Glasgow Herald* 2 March 1886

xii. *Belfast News Letter* 3 March 1886

xiii. *Hull Daily Mail* 12 March 1886

xiv. RNLI Inspector's Report Book F p411–412

xv. RNLI Inspector's Report Book F p412

Chapter 7: Swansong

i. *Belfast News Letter* 7 June 1888

ii. RNLI Inspector's Report Book I p365–366

iii. Ian Cameron *Riders of the Storm* (2002) p44

iv. ibid p 42

v. Oliver Warner *The Lifeboat Service* (1974) p33

vi. *Belfast News Letter* 18 January 1895

vii. Richard Lewis *A History of the Lifeboat* (1874) p79

viii. *Belfast Weekly News* 23 June 1888

ix. *Manchester Times* 13 November 1888

x. *Belfast News Letter* 3 January 1890
xi. Richard Lewis *A History of the Lifeboat* (1874)
     p 193–194
xii. *Northern Whig* 28 September 1894
xiii. *Belfast News Letter* 10 December 1898
xiv. Oliver Warner *The Lifeboat Service* (1974)
     p60–61
xv. *Saunders's News Letter* 3 February 1871

Chapter 8: Epitaph
i. *Belfast News Letter* 18 November 1899
ii. RNLI Inspector's Report Book F p368
iii. *Lifeboat Journal* Vol 4 Issue 39
iv. Speech made at the Annual General Meeting
    of the Royal National Lifeboat Institution
    in March 1876; as reported in *The Salisbury
    Times* 25 March 1876

Bibliography

Cameron, Ian — *Riders of the Storm: The Story of the RNLI*, London, Weidenfield & Nicolson (2002)

Cox, Barry — *Lifeboat Gallantry: The complete record of RNLI gallantry medals and how they were won 1824–1996*, London, Spink & Son (1998)

Dibdin, J C & Ayling, John — *The Book of the Lifeboat*, Edinburgh & London, Oliphant, Anderson & Ferrier (1894)

Harris, Walter — *The Ancient & Present State of the County Down*, Dublin (1744) Reproduced by Davidson Books, Ballynahinch

Kipling, Ray — *Rescue by Sail & Oar: Lifeboats before the Days of Engine Power*, Berkshire, Tops'l Books (1982)

Leach, Nicholas — *The Lifeboat Service in Ireland: station by station*, Stroud, Tempus (2005)

Lewis, Richard — *History of the Lifeboat & its works* (2nd edition), London, Macmillan & Co (1874)

Morris, Jeff — *Illustrated Guide to our Lifeboat Stations. Part 8: Ireland: with a brief history of every station, past and present.* Coventry, Lifeboat Enthusiasts Society (1993)

Mourne Observer — *Sailing Ships of Mourne: The County Down Fishing Fleet & Newcastle Lifeboat.* (reprinted from features published in the Mourne Observer) Newcastle, Co Down Mourne Observer Ltd, (1971)

Mundel, Frank	Stories of the Lifeboat (5th edition) London, the Sunday School Union (1894)
	Nautical Magazine & Naval Chronicle (1867), Cambridge University Press
RNLI	Lifeboat Journal, Fleet Street London, Charles Knight
RNLI	Committee Minutes (1850–1900) Case Numbers 674, 998 Inspector's Reports Books C,F,I Service Records: Tyrella Co Down Poole, RNLI Archives
Warner, Oliver	The Lifeboat Service: A History of the RNLI 1824–1974, London, Cassell & Company Ltd (1974)

List of Newspapers

Belfast Daily Mercury
Belfast Evening Telegraph
Belfast Morning News
Belfast News Letter
Cardiff Times
Daily Telegraph
Down Recorder
Downpatrick Recorder
Downshire Protestant
Dublin Daily Express
Dublin Evening Packet
Freeman's Journal
Glasgow Herald
Gloucester Citizen
Hull Daily Mail
Illustrated Times
Irish News
Lancashire Evening Post
Lloyd's Lists
London Evening Standard
Manchester Courier & Lancashire General Advertiser

Manchester Times
Morning Post
Mourne Observer
Newry Telegraph
Northern Whig
Oxford Times
St James' Gazette
Salisbury Times
Saunders's News Letter
Sheffield Daily Telegraph
Shipping and Mercantile Gazette
Southern Reporter & Cork Commercial Courier
Sunderland Daily Echo
The Scotsman
Vindicatory
Waterford Mail
Weekly Vindicator
Western Daily Press
www.britishnewspaperarchive.co.uk

Index